THE JEWISH PEOPLE

HISTORY • RELIGION • LITERATURE

THE JEWISH PEOPLE

HISTORY • RELIGION • LITERATURE

Advisory Editor
Jacob B. Agus

Editorial Board
Louis Jacob
Jacob Petuchowski
Seymour Siegel

MOSES MENDELSSOHN

Critic and Philosopher

H[ermann] Walter

ARNO PRESS
A New York Times Company
NEW YORK • 1973

Reprint Edition 1973 by Arno Press Inc.

Reprinted from a copy in
  The Newark Public Library

THE JEWISH PEOPLE: History, Religion, Literature
ISBN for complete set: 0-405-05250-2
See last pages of this volume for titles.

Manufactured in the United States of America

————◆————

Library of Congress Cataloging in Publication Data

Walter, Hermann, 1863-
  Moses Mendelssohn, critic and philosopher.

  (The Jewish people: history, religion, literature)
  Reprint of the 1930 ed. published by Bloch Pub. Co.,
New York.
  Bibliography: p.
  1. Mendelssohn, Moses, 1729-1786.   I. Series.
B2693.W3 1973   193 [B]   73-2230
ISBN 0-405-05291-X

MOSES MENDELSSOHN

Critic and Philosopher

MOSES MENDELSSOHN

(Painted by Anton Graff. Engraved by J. F. Bause)

MOSES MENDELSSOHN

Critic and Philosopher

By

H. WALTER

Department of Germanic Languages and Literature,
McGill University, Montreal

NEW YORK
BLOCH PUBLISHING CO.
1930

PRINTED IN THE UNITED STATES OF AMERICA

PREFACE

The object of this book is to offer the reader what the student of cultural movements ought to know of the life and works of this remarkable Jew, Moses Mendelssohn.

Germany celebrated last year the two-hundredth anniversary of his birth and it is hoped that some of those who have only a vague idea of Mendelssohn as the grandfather of the composer and the friend of Lessing may want to render their knowledge of the man himself more extensive.

With exception of a little volume of biographical fiction published on this continent no attempt has, to my knowledge, been made to bring the significance of Mendelssohn home to the English reader. Most of the material for the study of Mendelssohn is written in German and the works, with the exception of his *Phaedo*, have never been translated into English. This made numerous quotations from his more important works seem desirable.

My own more intimate acquaintance with Mendelssohn and his works goes back to the time of my preliminary studies on Heine during which all kinds of Jewish questions were continually obtruding themselves, necessitating a closer acquaintance with historical and cultural Judaism. I was at once strongly attracted by the charming and interesting personality of Mendelssohn. I recognized in him the most important pivotal point in the Jewish cultural evolution of modern times and was well repaid by a closer study of the man and his works. I should be pleased to think that, as the result, I may have contributed something towards the rational appreciation of a man whose achievements have not always been judged very critically.

The bibliography given at the end of this volume does not, of course, pretend to be complete. It is merely a list of some of the works consulted in this study. An exhaustive Mendelssohn bibliography would, according to Dr. Oko, Chief Librarian of the Hebrew Seminary, Cincinnati, comprise over two thousand items.

Of the illustrations two are published for the first time: Lips' very characteristic portrait of Lavater and Juel's portrait of Charles Bonnet, the latter an amusing and instructive contrast to the epithet "the little sneak" bestowed on him by Lessing.

My cordial thanks are due to Miss Bertha Meyer of the Department of Germanics for suggestions and criticism, also to Dr. Oko for the courteous and generous way in which he placed the Hebrew Seminary Library at my disposal during the writing of this study.

Montreal, October 1930.   H. W.

CONTENTS

LIST OF ILLUSTRATIONS

INTRODUCTION

THE JEWS AS A RACIAL, RELIGIOUS AND NATIONAL ENTITY

The personality of Moses Mendelssohn and the significance of his achievements are not only of general cultural interest, but are closely interwoven with the initial stages of Jewish emancipation in the eighteenth century. So much of his work is directly subservient to that movement and even those of his philosophical and literary essays which are apparently entirely detached from the question of emancipation are so eminently the first fruits of the will to achieve at least spiritual freedom that a survey of the cultural conditions of the Jews of his time seems inevitable. The problem of this emancipation was peculiarly perplexing, for emancipation meant more than a mere freeing from restraints imposed by an unsympathetic non-Jewish environment. That was its least important aspect. It involved in the foremost place a shaking off of chains of their own forging, of spiritual fetters the very nature of which seemed to preclude all prospect of even a moderate measure of cultural assimilation with the non-Jewish environment, an indispensable condition of improved civic relations.

The Jews claimed to be a separate religious community, a separate nationality and a race, which for thousands of years had miraculously been kept pure while all other races had become hopelessly contaminated by contact with each other. The pride the Jews took in their exclusiveness and the hostile attitude aroused by these claims among the Christians, who were compelled by their own scriptural authority to regard them as well-founded, drew the Jews even more closely together. Persecution, combined with a cultural vision rendered singularly myopic by the narrowness of their life in the ghetto, welded the German Jews into a compact mass possessing an apparently indestructible power of cohesion and a degree of impenetrability unheard of in the history of mankind. It seemed as hopeless to make any impression on this conglomerate of stubborn convictions and ubiquitous inhibitions as to try to break up a polished block of marble with one's fingernails.

The question whether the claim of purity of the Jewish race is well-founded or not need not detain us. Religious dogmas like national traditions may or may not fly in the face of observed facts and yet be extraordinarily potent for good or evil. The only thing that matters in this case is the fact that the Jews held this belief as a fundamental, axiomatic truth and that it exerted a strongly unifying influence over those who held it, compensating to some degree for the want of a common language.

Hebrew had ceased to be the vernacular of the Jews as early as their return from the Babylonian Exile and had become exclusively the language of literature and of prayer. After the Dispersion the Jews adopted the language of whatever country they chanced to inhabit. When in the fifteenth century, as the result of the ever-increasing persecution in Europe, most congregations were invaded by foreign elements, expelled from other places and speaking other languages, there resulted a number of jargons made up mainly of a dialect of the country invaded with an admixture of Hebrew words and a sprinkling from the vocabulary of the invader. Obviously, the limited regional intelligibility of these jargons, such as the Judeo-German or Yiddish, unfitted them for serving as a common national bond between the scattered portions of the people.

The situation of the Jews in the eighteenth century is peculiar. They are without a country and without a common language, and yet we may say that at no period of their history, not even in Palestine, had the feeling of national solidarity been stronger than it was then among the Jews throughout the world. If this feeling of solidarity be taken as a criterion they had at that time a better claim to be called a nation than the contemporary Germans. This was due to a common stock of cherished traditions of the past, of aspirations regarding the future and that greatest of unifying forces, persecution.

Most of these traditions owe their inspirational power to the Jewish religion. The practice of the Jews to invest everything, from great national achievements and catastrophes down to the most commonplace events of everyday life, with religious significance made it difficult, if not impossible, to separate Jewish life and religion and consider the one apart from the other. All their history thus became sacred history. Their national and religious traditions being merged into one became doubly unassailable and were invested with an irresistible potency of appeal.

Hand in hand with the traditions of a theocratic past went the Jewish faith in the glory of a theocratic future, in the appearance of a Messiah and the return of the Chosen People to Palestine, the coming of the Saviour being the indispensable condition of the restoration of the Jewish State. The strength of their faith may be gauged by the readiness with which any claimant for Messianic honours was hailed by the Jews. There have been at least fifteen. They did not all meet with the same measure of success. Some were of purely regional importance and influence, a few were obvious and transparent frauds whose reign was shortlived but there were others, such as Sabbatai Zevi, whose claim met with devout acceptance and recognition with the major portion of Jewry throughout the world.

If the Jews looked upon themselves as a racial, religious and national entity, this conviction was not only held as a matter of choice or of historical deduction but was forcibly and painfully impressed and imposed upon them by their Christian surroundings by means of persecution in all its forms from the cruellest to the meanest: death, torture, expulsion and humiliating restrictions. It is very unlikely that without such persecution Jewish orthodoxy, both religious and political, could for centuries have withstood the disintegrating influence of non-Jewish cultural contact. At all events there can be no reasonable doubt that persecution, painful though its consequences were to individuals, had one beneficent result for Judaism: it united the Jewish people as a whole and put off the evil day of disintegration and schism for centuries.

Among the humiliating restrictions imposed upon the Jews there were some purely childish ones such as the wearing of a peculiar garb. One, however, the Ghetto, was fraught with far-reaching consequences entirely unforeseen by the Jews themselves or their tormentors. Segregation was originally not imposed but arose out of the circumstances. It was perfectly natural that the Jews would for their own comfort and mutual protection prefer to live in Jewish surroundings and it was highly desirable that they should live near the synagogue, the school, the ritual bath and the various dealers in kosher foods. The mere surrounding of a portion of the town inhabited by them with a wall was not necessarily looked upon by them as an act of discrimination against them, seeing that at that time all towns were surrounded by walls. In some cases it must have appeared as a privilege rather than a hardship. The ghetto became a form of persecution only when the wall ceased to be a purely protective and became a restrictive device deliberately rendering the lives of the ever-increasing inhabitants more and more unbearable through the inevitable overcrowding of the very limited space marked off for their use. When, as a consequence of restricted intercourse with the Gentiles, there necessarily followed the ever-deepening ignorance regarding the Jews, the latter became the easy victims of all the dense ecclesiastical and social superstition of the age and their settlement was looked upon as a colony of lepers whose touch defiled the body and imperilled the soul. Besides, wholesale pillage and massacres were enormously facilitated by this convenient local concentration of the victims.[1]

The cultural consequences of this ghetto life were no less serious than the physical discomforts and dangers it entailed. The system of segregation began somewhere about the fifteenth century and was in full swing during the sixteenth, seventeenth and eighteenth centuries. Thus for three centuries, the most

---

[1] For almost incredible instances of the treatment of the Jews as late as the 16th & 17th centuries see B. H. Auerbach, *Geschichte der israelitischen Gemeinde Halberstadt.*

important in the history of mankind, the Jews, although living in Europe, were debarred from participating in the progress of European civilization, excluded from the great emancipation of the Renaissance, untouched by the stimulating clash of ideas of the great religious upheaval, the Reformation, with its insistence on the revolutionary principle of the periodic revaluation of religious values, and were forced to live their medieval life until the very end of the eighteenth century. When emancipation came at last they were compelled to swallow the rationalism of the time in such unwholesomely big doses that it threatened to become the undoing of Judaism.

A hostile environment could not but sharpen the mind of the Jew and develop in him a high degree of adaptability. It made him at once the most pliant and the most stubborn of men. Yet the general effect of the ghetto life on his mentality was deplorable "for whoever is condemned to live in the ghetto will gradually acquire the habit of thinking in the ghetto." [2] In the Middle Ages when most people, Jews as well as Christians, lived in an intellectual ghetto anyhow, segregation would not have mattered very much. Any difference would have been in favour of the Jews who could at least all read, a by no means universal accomplishment among their Christian contemporaries. But when the Renaissance began to

[2] Güdemann, *Geschichte der Erziehung und Kultur der Juden.*

dispel the darkness, its rays did not penetrate the
ghetto and it has even been said that when the Middle Ages came to an end for the rest of Europe they
began for the Jews.

Narrow and restricted like their habitat were their
daily occupation and their intellectual horizon. It
might happen locally that the Jews were allowed considerable freedom in the choice of a livelihood but,
generally speaking, we may say that in ghetto times
the Jews were allowed to engage only in occupations
in which they did not compete with Christians, such,
therefore, as were either too unpleasant or irksome,
like peddling, or were considered sinful like usury.
That as the result there was a general disposition to
take to the money business is natural enough seeing
that money was their only weapon of defence, the
only means of obtaining toleration and protection at
the hands of the state. The "Schutzjuden," the Jews
privileged to reside in specified towns, often added
considerably to the private income of individual
princes of Germany. Sometimes the prince claimed
for himself the exclusive right of "molesting" the
Jews with taxes [8] but generally the state and the civic
authorities managed to get some share in this scram-
ble for Jewish money. According to Auerbach the
Jews of Halberstadt were liable to pay fifteen different kinds of taxes in addition to the taxes paid

[8] B. H. Auerbach, *Geschichte der israelitischen Gemeinde
Halberstadt*, p. 24.

by non-Jews. When we add to this the cost of the upkeep of their many charitable enterprises and the periodical partial or total destruction of their possessions by their bigoted fellow-citizens, we can understand the anxiety of the Jews to engage in that form of business which promised the quickest and the most lucrative returns, i. e. moneylending.

Segregation offered few cultural compensations. The ghetto folksongs were far from exhilarating, they were wearisomely monotonous in their plaintive sadness. Nature plays no part in them. They originated exclusively in towns among town-dwellers for whom the comparative safety of the ghetto walls had greater charms than the finest landscape outside the city. The weather was probably the only aspect of nature that would interest the Jewish pedlar trudging along the country road with his heavy pack on his shoulders. The early marriage of mere boys and girls from the age of twelve upwards, negotiated and concluded strictly on business considerations, precluded all idea of love as sung by our poets.[4] The fine arts never brightened the squalid misery of the ghetto and all literature except works of religious import was taboo. Indeed, apart from a singularly pure and united home life, religion was the one redeeming feature of ghetto life. It took the place of everything that elsewhere makes life worth living

---

[4] See Pinès, *Histoire de la Littérature judéo-allemande;* also the very interesting *Memoirs* of Glückel von Hameln.

and so the paradoxical saying that the Jew is the product of Judaism is not merely plausible but literally true when applied to ghetto times.

Now the Jewish religion is so simple as to make a Jewish theology appear almost a luxury. Its metaphysical dogmas are few and so fundamental that they seem to supply the irreducible minimum of all religion. The feet of the orthodox Jew are planted on the solid earth, for his monotheism was mainly conditioned by political factors. It is preeminently practical. It has been defined as a system of political and hygienic ethics on which a supernatural eschatology had been grudgingly grafted at the time of the Babylonian Captivity. Not what a man believes is of importance but what he does.[5] It is a non-worrying religion. The Jew has nothing analogous to the doctrine of individual election, nor the sin against the Holy Ghost, nor any other theological puzzle likely to spring surprises on him in another world. He can verify at any moment of the day whether he has attained to righteousness or not, the minute fulfilment of the law being the one and only condition. Besides, Judaism recognizes no persons endowed with hierarchic power and authority. Priestcraft in the ordinary sense of the word had no terrors for the ghetto Jew. If the Jews in times of persecution and segregation were to keep their sanity this was pre-

[5] S. Schechter, *Studies in Judaism.*

cisely the kind of religion that would enable them to do so. It was free from all unbalancing dread and, as it contained very little mystic sand for the distressed soul to hide its head in, it left little scope, indeed hardly any excuse, for sectarianism and it enabled its adherents to attain to a degree of cohesion unheard of in the history of other religions.

If there is no theology in the ordinary sense of the word there is something to take its place, the Talmud, the chief recreation as well as the chief intellectual interest of the ghetto Jew, a monumental work explaining, illustrating and amplifying the law of Moses. As early as the thirteenth century, Asher ben Jischiel could not conceive how pious Jews could occupy themselves with matters outside the Talmud; and as late as the end of the eighteenth century a father could say to his son: "He who understands the Talmud understands everything." [6] This no doubt expressed the opinion of the great majority of the Jews up to the middle of the eighteenth century.

The Talmud proved at once a blessing and a curse. Before the time of the Renaissance the study of the Talmud raised the Jews immeasurably above the level of their mainly illiterate Christian surroundings. As for the succeeding centuries the best that can be said is that it was probably better that the Jews should study the Talmud than nothing at all, for the pos-

[6] Salomon Maimon's *Autobiography*.

session and intensive study of that work during ghetto times prevented the Jews from degenerating into a mere rabble of pedlars and moneylenders and kept alive among them a love of higher things. On the other hand, its retarding and narrowing influence —binding and garotting the intellect as Leroy-Beaulieu puts it—is equally certain. It has been well said that the ghetto had two walls, one built by the city and the other by the Talmud.

From being a mere commentary of the Law of Moses the Talmud soon began to partake of the sacred character of the commented text. It was studied not only by grown-up Jews as a religious duty and a recreation but it was practically the only thing taught in schools.

Elementary schools in the eighteenth century, Jewish or Christian, were nothing to be proud of anywhere. In most parts of Germany, teachers for Christian schools were often recruited from among unsuccessful tradesmen or the coachmen and other servants of country squires, superannuated for drunkenness or other forms of unfitness. They were often incredibly coarse, brutal and ignorant. Jewish schools were probably several degrees worse than Christian schools. According to Cohen,[7] the teacher rarely had any other qualification except his unfitness for other callings relieved by unblemished piety. Strass-

[7] I. Cohen, *Jewish Life in Modern Times.*

burger [8] and Fromer [9] give lurid details regarding the personality of the teachers and the unsanitary condition of the schools. The curriculum could not possibly have been narrower. Ability to read the Talmud was the sole aim. That most of the teachers hailed from Poland was probably responsible for this, as in Poland the Talmud study had developed into a perfect craze. Every Polish Jew was a Talmud scholar or trying to become one. In the whole of Poland there was scarcely a Jewish household in which the Talmud was not studied by some member. Even in congregations of only fifty members there would be, according to Strassburger, as many as twenty Talmud scholars instructing the remaining thirty. The study of the Talmud was considered to be the most meritorious occupation a man could engage in to the neglect of every other duty. Fromer tells us how his father used to rise at four in the morning to go to the Club of the Chassidim and spend the whole day in prayer and the study of the Talmud while his wife earned the money for the family by peddling. Fromer adds that his father, from his earliest youth, knew of no occupation beyond the study of the Talmud and the maintenance of good relations with God. The Talmud scholar was

[8] Strassburger, *Geschichte der Erziehung und des Unterrichts bei den Israeliten.*
[9] Fromer, *Vom Ghetto zur modernen Kultur.*

by far the most acceptable son-in-law and Salomon
Maimon relates in his *Autobiography* how, because
at the age of eleven he showed uncommon skill in
Talmudic disputations, he was waylaid by pro-
spective parents-in-law and ultimately literally kid-
napped and carried off in triumph by a woman who
wanted him to marry her daughter.

As carried on by Polish Jews the study of the
Talmud developed in the devotees incredible skill in
setting up and solving intricate problems. In the art
of hairsplitting and quibbling they attained to a
proficiency undreamed of before their time. Naturally their method of Talmudic study was everywhere
followed by intellectual barrenness. The best heads
were enticed away from serious studies where mere
arid dialectics had no opportunities of winning
laurels. Yet it was really not so much intelligence that
was required for Talmudic dialectics as rather a pre-
ternaturally quick and ever-ready low cunning such
as one wants for finding the solution of charades,
puzzles and trigonometrical problems. A further result was the vanishing of all real interest in the
biblical record, the simplicity and straightforward-
ness of which had no charms to attract the Talmudist.
The Pentateuch was still used for liturgical purposes
and thus received its mead of veneration which,
however, was more or less a matter of national tradition and habit. Nothing shows more conclusively the
withering effect of this Talmudic craze than the fact

that no Jewish literature could arise, let alone flourish, under this régime, and that neo-Hebrew and Yiddish could become literary languages only after the Reform movement had done its work and exorcised the Polish incubus.[10]

Jewish belles-lettres had always been singularly narrow in scope. From the almost exclusively agricultural Jews in ancient Palestine nothing else could be expected, and their descendants in Europe fashioned their literature mainly on biblical models and seemed to be afraid of roaming beyond the sacred precincts. While in two other countries, Spain and Italy, due to foreign influences, an extension beyond these narrow biblical limits was attempted, German Jewry at no period of its history succeeded in cutting the leading strings of tradition. Indeed in the eighteenth century the field of intellectual activity was still further restricted until their literature became a mere literature of interpretation of the formalism of past ages, concerning itself entirely with rules of conduct of so minute and hairsplitting a character, so purely intellectual in their appeal that broad ethical principles were completely lost sight of and all sense of proportion vanished.

It was, of course, not to be expected that all Jews without exception would meekly submit to this spiritual tyranny. At a time like the eighteenth century,

[10] See N. Slouschz, *Renascence of Hebrew Literature,* and A. G. Waldstein, *Evolution of Modern Hebrew Literature.*

not an age of excessive meekness, this was inconceivable. German Jews were not all living in ghettoes and even the walls of the ghetto could not and did not prevent all contact between Jews and the world outside. In spite of rabbinical opposition, profane literature was smuggled into the Jewish community. The Oppenheim Library, now incorporated in the Bodleian, showed in 1740 in the Jewish-German section, no fewer than 380 works, a not inconsiderable portion of which is made up of profane literature of non-Jewish origin.[11] Just as the Renaissance corroded the power of the Church by the mere fact that it showed Europe a view of life differing fundamentally from that set up by the Catholic Church, which Europe had settled down to believing was the only possible one, the non-Jewish literature invading the ghetto proved the first of the disintegrating influences which led to the downfall of Polish rabbinism and the Talmudic idol. It showed in no matter how naïve a manner the possibility of a life more complex and more satisfying than that of the Talmudist.

Many Jews who were not compelled to live in a ghetto, or who though living there were by their business brought into frequent contact with the cultured portion of the outside world, felt keenly the intellectual and emotional limitations imposed upon

[11] R. P. Frankl, "Erbauungs-und Unterhaltungslektüre unserer Altvordern." *Monatsschrift für Geschichte und Wissenschaft des Judenthums.* 1885.

them. These really proved harder to bear than civic disabilities which they shared in any case with a great many non-Jewish Germans. Everything around them was in a state of ferment; literature, political ideas, social relations, education and religion were thrown in the melting pot. The glaring contrast between the colossal ideas of the time and the meanness and narrowness of Jewish life was both ludicrous and pathetic. Besides, it was obvious that the time was gone for any body of men to exclude themselves from the common destiny of surrounding humanity and to lead a mental, social and political life apart from their fellowmen. In this cataclysmic upheaval it was physically impossible for any portion of the area affected to remain stagnant. The Jews had to be drawn into the vortex of modern evolution or disappear altogether as a cultural factor.

How was this modernization of the Jews to be brought about? As long as the preservation of Judaism was the only thing that mattered, as long as this could be attained only by every Jew being a "good" Jew, segregation was felt as an advantage, but the increasing intercourse between Jews and Christians due to scepticism, the spread of religious indifference in the Christian camp and the consequent inevitable breaking down of prejudice and intolerance made the harmful cultural implications of the ghetto only too apparent. The cultural differences between Jew and Gentile was abysmal; even the language the Jew spoke excited nothing but ridicule and contempt.

Now there is nothing more stubborn and hidebound in its conservatism than a Talmudic Jew, nothing so hopelessly impervious to the appeals of the reformer, and as in the latter portion of ghetto times practically all Jews were Talmudic Jews, it was highly improbable that any radical change would come from within. There had, of course, always been individual instances of more or less open doubters, chiefly among Italian and Portuguese Jews, some of them well known, such as Luzzato, Delmedigo and Acosta who dared to point out the weakness of the dominant form of Judaism, but generally went no further, and in most cases did not feel called upon to suggest remedial measures and thus incur the penalties few reformers can escape. Where, as in the case of Acosta, something more was attempted and criticism manifested itself as an actual infraction of the Talmudic Law, orthodox Judaism did not hesitate a moment and mercilessly crushed the rebel. The solid wall of Jewish orthodoxy against which some of the rasher rebels broke their heads was all the more impenetrable as there was no separate priesthood to deal with and the recalcitrant member of the flock had to defend himself against a vague and elusive enemy, a crowd. The dreaded sentence of excommunication was pronounced by the council of elders representing the congregation. The excommunicated could then choose between two evils, starvation or conversion to Christianity. Often the offender was exiled by the Christian authorities for these were only too ready to take advantage of the chance of expelling Jews whom the Jews themselves would not have. Even Spinoza with all his great qualities of intellect and character failed to make the slightest impression on Judaism. It would have been surprising if it had been otherwise as he had not the faintest intention to reform Judaism. He simply had no use for it. This want of appreciation was mutual so that when we say the Jews gave us Spinoza, this is literally true as they did not want him themselves.

After the time of Spinoza the unquestioned sway of Talmudic Judaism seemed to be assured for ever. If there was any opposition it remained inarticulate. It was the silence of the graveyard. Judaism as a living force was dead without knowing it. Never had Judaism sunk lower than in the period of about a hundred years following the excommunication of Spinoza. It was a nightmare of narrowness and superstition, "a time," as Graetz says, "when the Jews, the former teachers of Europe, became dotards and every public act of the Jews bore the character of imbecility." They still had their national virtues to commend them: chastity, family love and sympathy towards one another. The rest was pitiable. Well might Mendelssohn write to Hemmings: "My people are kept so far apart from culture that one might well despair of the possibility of improvement."

Spinoza had died in 1677. It was not till nearly a century later that the publication of Mendelssohn's *Phaedo* again drew attention to the Jews as a people still to be reckoned with in the evolution of European thought.

I

EARLY YEARS

Moses Mendelssohn was born on the 6th of September, 1729, in Dessau whence he derived the name he originally bore, Moses Dessau. Mendelssohn himself tells us very little about his early years. Probably there was little enough to tell. He was a puny, delicate boy and, in any case, the life of the Jewish child was so narrowly circumscribed that there was hardly any room for even such mild adventures as light up the boyhood story of ordinary people. We know that his father earned his living by copying Torah-scrolls and as an elementary teacher, neither to be counted among the lucrative professions. The demand for Torah-scrolls was probably never very brisk and an elementary teacher's income was always despicably small and often hard to collect. Of his mother nothing is known except that she died before her son attained to fame and that her name was Suschen, but this paucity of material does not prevent some biographers from giving their readers a glowing description of the lovable woman she must have been and the exact traits of character her son owed to her.

If we know little of Mendelssohn's parents we do not know much more of the Jewish colony in Dessau. The first Jews seem to have settled there about the last quarter of the preceding century. Beyond the assurance that they were granted privileges greatly superior to those enjoyed in adjoining principalities, we know nothing of the relations of Jews and Christians in Dessau.[1] The place seems to have been something like a Jewish intellectual centre judging by the circumstance that it possessed a Jewish printing press capable of producing a reprint of Maimon's *Moreh Nebuchim,* also that Jewish scholars flocked to the place for the printing of their own works and for study and were hospitably received at the local Bet ha-Midrash. The very learned chief rabbi of the congregation, David Hirschel Fränkel, was no doubt another great attraction.

It has never been the custom of Jewish parents to neglect the education of their children on the plea of poverty. Rather we might say the poorer the parents the greater their anxiety that their children should "learn," not that they might achieve success in life but that they might become "good" Jews in the first place and, if possible, scholars. Nevertheless the children were not to be envied, for their studies, especially those of the brainy ones, were exceedingly strenuous. There was no kindergarten to provide a

[1] For what little is known of the Jews in Dessau see L. Würdig and B. Hesse: *Die Dessauer Chronik.*

THE MENDELSSOHN HOUSE IN DESSAU
(*Photo by Fula, Dessau*)

pleasantly greased inclined plane from the playfulness and the freedom of the nursery to the seriousness of life; boys of five were taken by the scruff of the neck and plunged into the study of one of the hardest languages, Hebrew.

So young was Moses when he first went to school that often on cold winter days his father had to wrap the sickly boy in a cloak and carry him there. When he reached the age of six he was transferred to a higher school, the Bet ha-Midrash, where he was initiated into the study of the Talmud. At the age of ten he wrote Hebrew poetry, excellent according to some, but as he burned these poems before long, we are justified in concluding that they stood considerably lower in his own opinion than in that of his friendly critics. What is more significant is that before he was thirteen the Hebrew version of Maimon's *Moreh Nebuchim* (Guide of the Perplexed) had become his *livre de chevet*. Maimon attempts to explain Judaism solely by an appeal to reason and was thus a forerunner of the religious rationalism of the eighteenth century. The work had long ago been placed under the ban by the orthodox. Printers, editors and readers ran the risk of being accused of heresy. As the book was nevertheless reprinted by the Dessau press and its reading by Moses countenanced and actively aided by the Chief Rabbi of the place, we may be sure that Dessau was at the time not seriously contaminated by Polish orthodoxy. It was a

great stroke of luck that the boy was born at Dessau,
for one shudders to think what might have become of
this young glutton had he fallen into the blighting
hands of a Polish Talmudist.

While the study of Maimon's philosophy of religion undoubtedly laid the foundation of Mendelssohn's religious rationalism and made of him one
of the champions of so-called natural religion, the
precocious student's unremitting industry and almost
fanatical devotion to the study of this work still
further debilitated a body already unduly handicapped. He suffered a severe illness from the effects
of which he probably never entirely recovered. Besides, the curvature of the spine with which he was
born had now developed into a regular unsightly
hump as the result of his excessive stooping over his
books. "I owe it to Maimon," he used to say, "that I
have such a misshapen body; he alone is the cause of
it; but I love him nevertheless for he has sweetened
many a bitter hour of my life and has thus compen-
sated me tenfold for what damage he has done to my
body."

A Jew, poor, sickly, a hunchback and moreover
afflicted with a distressing stammer: what an equipment for the strenuous struggle for life amidst the
unsympathetic rabble he was sure to encounter on his
way!

When Moses was thirteen his parents could no
longer bear the burden of maintaining him. He would

have to shift for himself. There was no need for calling a family council and wasting time on deliberations as to the best way of achieving his independence. The boy must either marry and expect his parents-in-law, according to the common Jewish custom, to provide the means for carrying on his studies by looking after his housing, feeding and clothing— a popular and inexpensive way of getting an education among the Jews of that time [2]—or he must earn his own living. As he was sickly and deformed the prospect of the former alternative coming his way did not seem very bright, for obvious reasons he could not become a moneylender. He was thus reduced to taking up the profession requiring a minimum of capital and giving quick returns, peddling.

We do not know whether he actually went out with his pack and none of his biographers have as yet thought of adding to our store of legendary matter relating to Mendelssohn's life by picturing the author of *Phaedo* selling pots and pans and haggling with the housewives in the villages about Dessau. It is very improbable that he ever carried even the lightest of packs. In any case we know that sooner or later he succeeded in persuading his parents to let him study a little longer.

[2] Cf. Salomon Maimon's *Autobiography*.

II

FIRST YEARS IN BERLIN

The learned Rabbi Fränkel, who had hitherto
guided him through the mazes of Hebrew language
and hermeneutics, had meanwhile received a call as
Chief Rabbi to Berlin. The poor boy felt lost; he was
like a ship without a pilot and a few months later
Moses had wormed the permission to go to Berlin
out of his parents. With a courage born partly of a
total ignorance of the difficulties besetting his path
and partly of an unflinching determination to achieve
his end the fourteen year old boy set out on his way.
He did the whole journey from Dessau to Berlin, a
matter of about eighty miles, on foot we may suppose, and arrived at the Rosenthal Gate, the only one
by which Jews were allowed to enter. The story of
the picturesque and pathetic scene supposed to have
been enacted when the pale little Jewish boy stam-
mered his request for admission, a story copied by
many biographers from Stern's *Geschichte des
Judentums,* is unfortunately not authentic.[1] That

[1] J. Auerbach, "Moses Mendelssohn und das Judentum."
Zeitschrift für die Geschichte der Juden in Deutschland. Bd. I.
1887.

he really did have an anxious ten minutes at the gate
is probable. He was at the mercy of a Jewish official
charged with the duty of keeping out undesirables and
the boy must surely have looked as if he was likely
to be a burden on the Jewish community which the
one ducat in his pocket would do little to lighten.
Possibly the mention of the name of Rabbi David
Fränkel under whom he wished to study favourably
impressed the Jewish Cerberus who thereupon allowed some of the regulations governing admission to
fall into temporary oblivion, and the boy slipped
through.

The Berlin of the reign of Frederick the Great was
by no means the Jewish paradise one might have
expected to find under the *roi philosophe,* who, while
he allowed every one of his subjects to attain salvation in another world in any way he pleased, held
some particularly stubborn views on the way they
were to attain happiness in this world and particularly
the maximum of happiness to be attained by the Jews.
His ancestors had never shown any marked predilection for the Chosen People and Frederick the
Great disliked them even more. Not that it would be
possible to lay any particular oppressive act to his
charge, but no attempt was made to abrogate restrictions which were becoming unbearable, partly no
doubt through the fault of the Jews themselves, who,
in Berlin as so often elsewhere, did a great deal of
the Jew-baiting themselves. The selection and ad-

mission of the limited number of Jewish families who could settle in Berlin was more or less in the hands of the Jews themselves, a power which they used mainly with a view to maintaining a proper standard of religious intolerance within the community. No Jewish author from another city could solicit subscriptions for any work he was about to publish without the consent of the Jewish religious authorities. The reading of non-Jewish literature was taboo and such a crime as carrying a German book on the street was punished with expulsion from the city, the Jewish authorities subtly concluding that the carrying of the book would sooner or later be followed by the reading of it.[2] The innumerable forms of physical annoyance and vexation, of the meanest injustice and the exorbitant financial exactions to which the state subjected the Jews were really less serious than the spiritual ghetto the Berlin Jews had created for themselves. To this must be added the contempt and detestation in which the Jews were held as a matter of tradition. A particularly telling instance of the latter is to be found in the terms of the decree regarding the Merchants' Guild issued in 1716 and in force not only during the reign of Frederick the Great but as late as 1802. "As the Merchants' Guild," we read, "is to be composed of honest and honourable persons, the following must be debarred from membership: Jews, homicides, blasphemers, murderers, thieves,

---

[2] L. Geiger, *Geschichte der Juden in Berlin.*

perjurers, adulterers or any other persons afflicted with great public vices or sins." With hatred, contempt and injustice on the side of the Christians, deep resentment and the conviction of their own superiority on the side of the Jews, there was no need of a ghetto wall to keep the two apart.

Into this arena of petty strife, ignorance and prejudice young Mendelssohn came from the calm and peaceful atmosphere of his native Dessau. It is unlikely that he became aware of the difference from the very first. On his arrival he steered straight for the friendly haven of Rabbi Fränkel's house and for some time to come he led such a retired life and was so absorbed by his studies that he hardly had time to become cognizant of his surroundings. Fränkel was somewhat embarrassed by his arrival; he had enough problems on hand, most Jewish congregations supply their rabbis with these without stint, and he was not looking for further trouble at the time. He did what he could for him which was just sufficient for the lad to keep body and soul together by a few slender threads represented by a chilly and ill-lighted garret a coreligionist placed at his disposal, a few free meals a week at different houses and a few groschen for copying work. His breakfast, supper and some of his dinners consisted of dry bread and even that in famine rations. Going to bed hungry was by no means a rare occurrence at that time. What kept up his courage was merely his desire to learn, knowledge without any ulterior aim in view such as wealth, fame or power which have so often enabled young lads to undergo incredible privations. It was an idealistic attitude characteristic of many ghetto Jews.

Mendelssohn would no doubt at first take up his Jewish studies where he had left them off at Dessau, but soon he realized that a purely Jewish education would not quench his thirst for knowledge so he sought other springs. His mother tongue had been Yiddish and he had hitherto spoken Yiddish exclusively, a cruel handicap in a German-speaking community. It was inevitable that to his inquisitive mind German should appear to be the key to treasures of knowledge unattainable without it. Fortunately uncompromising orthodoxy invariably breeds the dissenting bacillus that will ultimately undermine it, just as some of our insect pests are destroyed by the parasites bred and burrowing in their own bodies. In this Jewish community, which took such meticulous care to preserve its orthodoxy pure and undefiled, the enemy, none the less dangerous because hidden, had secured a foothold. There were Jews in Berlin so far fallen from grace that they read and possessed German books, secretly no doubt as the respectable Englishman of last generation used to read his yellow-back French novels, but in addition with a sense of the very real risk he was running if one of the spying elders should catch him at it. Borrowing such books no matter what their contents, provided they were in German, was obviously the impecunious youth's only way to get the material for his study of the language. That one of the first books through which he plodded laboriously was Reinbeck's *Betrachtungen über die Augsburgische Konfession,* the very title of which would have frightened away most boys of his age, is characteristic of the haphazard way he stumbled across his reading. Still the work proved valuable as it made him acquainted with an entirely new field of knowledge, Christian theology, and it was doubly welcome as the philosophical part dealing with the proofs for the existence of the Deity seemed a modern continuation of the disquisitions of his beloved Maimon on the same subject.

Mendelssohn learnt the language without much method, without such aids as grammars and dictionaries. It is doubtful if a Yiddish-German dictionary existed at the time. It was backbreaking work, for though the Yiddish vocabulary contains about 80% of words of German origin and a knowledge of it is clearly an asset where merely the understanding of German is concerned, it is a millstone around the learner's neck and in many cases an insuperable obstacle where speaking and writing German is the object in view. Yiddish has practically no declensions, no simple past tense, no subjunctive, the prepositions govern no definite cases and dependent clauses have lost their characteristic word order. Besides, its vocalic and even some of its consonantal values differ essentially from those of German. Its resemblance to German is a trap for the unwary and many cultured Jews, whose early years were spent in a Yiddish milieu, never succeed in ridding themselves entirely of the linguistic habits of their youth. It borders on the miraculous that Mendelssohn should have mastered the German language so perfectly that he ultimately wrote it more elegantly than Lessing and that Kant could hold up his philosophical language as a model to be imitated by all philosophers.

Mendelssohn now had the good fortune to make the acquaintance of some of the black sheep of the Jewish flock, men who dared to engage in the pursuit of profane knowledge. One of them, Israel Samosz, had been driven from his native country, Galicia, for engaging in non-Talmudic studies. He initiated Mendelssohn in the study of mathematics, while Dr. Abraham Kisch, another refugee from the Jewish intolerance of Eastern Europe, taught him Latin which was then still the language in which many scientific and especially philosophical treatises were written. Dr. Aaron Salomon Gumpertz, who enjoys the distinction of having been the first Jew to receive a doctor's degree at a Prussian university, completed the young man's linguistic equipment by instructing him in French and English.

We may assume that by this time the glamour of Talmudic studies had become somewhat dimmed in his eyes, though he never ceased to interest himself in what had been the intellectual delight of his early years. At the same time his mentality was undergoing a change which might sooner or later bring him into perilous conflict with his more hide-bound co-religionists. If he enjoyed a pleasant immunity during the first seven years of his life in Berlin during which he had no sort of legal status, being neither a privileged Jew nor in the employ of a Jew entitled to reside in the city, this was probably owing to the sheltering obscurity and seclusion in which he carried on his nefarious practices and the harmless insignificance of his appearance. When many years later he published his German translation of the Pentateuch to the horror and indignation of Polish die-hards, his position in the Jewish world had become so exalted that their vindictive protests could no longer harm him.

At last after seven years of discomfort and privations of all kinds, Moses received the reward of his industry and tenacity. In 1750 a rich Berlin silk manufacturer, Isaac Bernhard, offered him the post of tutor to his children. The mean, sordid and miserly life came to an end, and he had now considerable leisure to devote to his studies. Nor must we forget that being now in the service of a privileged Jew he ceased to be outside the law; he was no longer a vagrant, liable to be expelled at any moment.

As the outcome of natural inclination as well as ot

the early training he received at the hands of Rabbi
Fränkel and of the introduction to more modern philosophy which he owed to Dr. Gumpertz, his main interest became centred on philosophic studies. Some
time before 1750, when he had barely mastered the
rudiments of Latin, he picked up a second hand copy
of a Latin translation of Locke's *Essay on the Human Understanding*. This he tackled and pored over
with the help of a wretched Latin dictionary bought
with his savings at a time when his total revenue
amounted to a few groschen a week. The result of unspeakable drudgery and no doubt of a good deal of
guessing was a working acquaintance with a philosopher who strongly appealed to him, possibly on account of the close relationship between that writer's
sensuous philosophy and the sensuous religion of the
Jews. Locke's denial of innate ideas and insistence on
the principle that all our knowledge comes from
experience and through our senses was no doubt
grist to the mill of a future champion of natural
religion with its denial of the necessity of revelation. Moreover, the fact that Locke had advocated
the abolition of Jewish disabilities would render
the philosopher's personality all the more sympathetic. That the comforting teleological harmony
of all things of Leibnitz should win his kind heart
almost as much as his head is equally intelligible.
Goethe's dictum that the result of our thinking is
more or less conditioned by our character is specially

applicable to the case of Mendelssohn in view of the decided ethical bias of his judgment. We experience greater difficulty in understanding his life-long enthusiasm for the arid dry-as-dust philosophy of Wolff. Did it set his heart strings vibrating by reminding him of the Talmudic methods of his earlier years?

III

MENDELSSOHN FINDS A MENTOR

Mendelssohn had now garnered a considerable store
of knowledge, not sufficiently intensive in any one
direction to amount to erudition, but extensive
enough to furnish the tools for serious literary and
philosophical investigation. As he was mainly self-
taught, however, there was a danger that this knowledge would continue to become more and more extensive rather than intensive and that his work would
ultimately bear the stamp of the shallow polyhistor.
His very thirst for knowledge was fraught with
danger. Moreover his poverty was a continual temptation to buy the books within his slender means rather
than the works he really ought to have bought to
deepen his knowledge. The recently reprinted cata-
logue of the books of his library [1] seems to confirm
this suspicion. What he needed above all things now
was a friend capable of sensing the promise of great
things under the cloak of shyness, awkwardness and
physical insignificance. He needed a scholarly guide

[1] *Verzeichnis der auserlesenen Bücherversammlung des seligen Herrn Moses Mendelssohn.* Brockhaus, Soncino-Gesellschaft.

who could encourage him to concentrate his mind on
the solution of definite problems, a writer of sufficiently established reputation whose influence would
smooth the obscure Jew's path to literary recognition.
Such a man he found in Lessing whom he met for the
first time in 1754. His teacher, Dr. Gumpertz, had
introduced Mendelssohn as an excellent chessplayer.
His real motive was no doubt a higher one: it was a
liberal education to know Lessing and Gumpertz felt
that the preliminary training he had given his pupil
had fitted him to benefit by such education now.

Lessing had at this period none of his great
achievements to his credit. A few comedies, a couple
of problem plays like *Der Freigeist* and *Der Jude*
make up the list of his poetic works; the rest had been
mainly philological and critical. What had contributed
most to his reputation was his literary criticism in
Beiträge zur Historie und Aufnahme des Theaters
and the *Vossische Zeitung*. But if the modest position he occupied in German literature was not for a
moment to be compared with the one that became his
due after *Laokoon, Emilia Galotti* and *Nathan,* he
was at least known as a controversial writer, an extraordinarily well informed and courageous journal-
ist, without pity for obviously incurable mediocrity
but endowed with unerring judgment for what was
really good or likely to become so. His critical method
was in sharp contrast to that of his contemporaries
which was either nauseating in its hosannahs or re-

volting in its ignorant destructiveness. With regard
to questions of religious and racial discrimination he
had made his position perfectly clear in his comedy
Der Jude or as he called it later *Die Juden*. The latter
title shows more emphatically the tendential character of the little work which apart from this character has no merit whatever. It achieved its main
purpose which was to allow Lessing to unburden himself on the subject of racial intolerance. A Jew has
been the means of delivering a country nobleman out
of the hands of two murderous villains. He is hospitably entertained by the baron whose gratitude finds
expression in the proposal that his benefactor should
marry his daughter. Then the horrid secret is revealed: his gallant rescuer, with a minimum of
alacrity, confesses that he is a Jew. In spite of the
"Well, what of that?" of the maiden, this ends the
matter. "How estimable the Jews would be if they
all resembled you!" exclaims the baron which the
Jew counters by saying: "How amiable the Christians
would be if they all possessed your virtues."

It was the first time that a virtuous and cultured
Jew appeared in German Literature. The effect was
disconcerting. Even the very liberal-minded Dr.
Michaelis of Göttingen felt perturbed by this portrait
of a perfectly good and highly cultured Jew. He con-
fessed in his review of the play in the *Göttinger
Gelehrte Anzeigen* that such a Jew was indeed possible but, he hastened to add, highly improbable, as

even ordinary virtue and probity were rarely met with among the Jews. In view of their ethical principles, he says, even common probity was hardly possible, particularly as nearly the whole nation was compelled to live by a trade which offers so many more opportunities and temptations to commit fraud than other occupations.

It is clear that in associating more closely, both Lessing and Mendelssohn defied the prejudices of their coreligionists, Lessing by his open recognition of the Jew as an equal and Mendelssohn by his equally unhesitating rupture with rabbinical exclusiveness. There was nothing provocative about the shy and reserved Mendelssohn's attitude but Lessing was triumphant. Before long he wrote to Michaelis, who a few years earlier had doubted the probability of a Jew being as noble as the hero in Lessing's comedy: "It is quite true that Mendelssohn is a Jew. He is a man of about twenty years of age who, without any instruction, has attained to advanced proficiency in the study of Languages, Mathematics, Philosophy and Poetry. If his own coreligionists will only allow him to develop in his own way, I predict that he will become an honour to his nation which has, however, always acted in an unfortunate spirit of persecution towards people of his type. His candour and his philosophic genius lead me to anticipate in him a second Spinoza who lacks only the errors of the latter to make him his complete equal." Lessing's fears as to the attitude of orthodox Judaism were not entirely groundless as shown by subsequent events, but he allowed his youthful optimism to run away with his judgment in the matter of Spinoza's mantle. It is not likely that twenty-five years later, when he knew a great deal more about Mendelssohn, he would have committed the same error.

The acquaintance with Lessing meant not only Lessing himself and all that name implied but the whole of the literary coterie surrounding him. While a number of Lessing's friends no doubt owed what fame they had entirely to their association with Lessing, others like Ramler and Nicolai stood on a pedestal of their own. By the time Lessing left Berlin towards the end of 1755, Mendelssohn was recognized as a man worth knowing and was readily admitted to the membership of the closed society of a coffeehouse established about 1755, frequented mainly by men of learning interested in Physics, Mathematics and Metaphysics, some of them of the distinction of the mathematician Euler.

IV

WINNING HIS SPURS

The first fruits of the friendship between Mendelssohn and Lessing are the *Philosophical Dialogues* (Philosophische Gespräche). The theme was suggested by Lessing who to give his friend a pleasant surprise had the work published without the knowledge of the author. It is of little importance to remember that the philosophical value of these Dialogues is very small. The very attempt to reconcile Spinoza and Leibnitz was a metaphysical *tour de force* that was not likely to yield any positive results. Two things interest us mainly: the phenomenal progress in the German language made by Mendelssohn who only a few years before had had to learn German almost as one learns a foreign language and his courageous defence of the personal character of Spinoza, the outcast from the Jewish fold, whose very name was still held in abhorrence by pious Jews. He admired Spinoza's personality, he marvelled at his extraordinary intellect, the boldness and depth of his conceptions, but he strongly, indeed indignantly, repudiated Spinoza's conclusions. He looked upon him as "the unfortunate victim of philosophical developments."

Mendelssohn never overcame the positive horror with which Pantheism filled him. When many years later he was told that his friend Lessing had been an avowed Pantheist, he died from the shock the news gave him.

All that characterizes Mendelssohn's philosophical work is already to be seen in his first treatise : his unshakable faith in the infallibility of the Leibnitz-Wolffian system, his desire to apply metaphysical principles to everyday life until their degree of applicability becomes almost a criterion of truth in his eyes. In this, of course, he was merely an interpreter of the prevailing philosophic current of thought, the so-called *Common Sense Philosophy,* the interest of which was centred on the ethical, philanthropic and humanitarian aspects of even the abstrusest questions of metaphysics. This expression of all philosophy in terms of ethics no doubt made it more accessible to the common man, but at the same time it limited the scope of philosophic inquiry. Logic and Epistemology, for instance, obstinately refuse to bend the neck under the ethical yoke. An unfortunate result of this ethical attitude was the tendency to make the personal character of the thinker participate in the reprobation meted out to his thought if it proved antagonistic to the supposed primary object of philosophy, the happiness of mankind, obviously a relic of the common theological superstition that unless a man hold the true faith he cannot possibly be moral. When Mendelssohn encounters Spinoza, a man of exemplary moral conduct who yet does not believe in a personal Deity, a belief, according to Mendelssohn, essential to the happiness of mankind, he is frankly puzzled. His intellectual honesty, however, compels him to append to his condemnation of Spinoza's philosophy a panegyric of his morals. He does not attempt an explanation of what to him is a contradiction and he has to leave his no doubt equally non-plussed readers to reconcile the facts as best they can.

The friendship between Mendelssohn and Lessing was still further cemented by a treatise written and published by them conjointly. The President of the Berlin Academy of Sciences, one of the pet schemes of Frederick II, was Maupertuis. He was exceedingly vain, hypersensitive and cantankerous and, as the result, everlastingly involved in literary, scientific and personal feuds, to which he partly owes his renown. The most famous of his scandals is his quarrel with another scientist, Samuel Koenig, which Voltaire summed up in a cruel diatribe against Maupertuis, *Histoire du Docteur Akakia.* That Maupertuis implored the protection of the King of Prussia who ordered a copy of the diatribe to be publicly burnt by the hangman probably only made matters worse, for the impression was inevitable that in imposing this medieval form of punishment on a book the King must have had his tongue in his cheek. Hardly had this humiliating incident been forgotten when Maupertuis asked for further trouble. For some time the fame of Leibnitz of whom he had always been envious had been keeping him awake at night. He could think of no better way to damage the philosopher's reputation than to persuade the Academy to offer a prize for the best essay on the *Philosophic System of Pope*. Among other points to be treated was a comparison of Pope and Leibnitz from which, as the President's attitude towards Leibnitz was well known to the competitors, Maupertuis' spitefulness expected much grim satisfaction. Lessing and Mendelssohn effectively turned the tables on Maupertuis by publishing in 1755 a little treatise, *Pope, a Metaphysician!* (Pope ein Metaphysiker!) "Who is Pope?" they asked, "a poet—a poet? What is Saul doing among the prophets? What is a poet doing among the metaphysicians?" Whereupon they show that as the object of poetry and of metaphysics is different, as are also the means employed by poet and metaphysicians to obtain their end, the poet cannot as a poet, and certainly does not in this case, evolve a metaphysical system. There cannot therefore be a comparison possible between the poet Pope and the metaphysician Leibnitz, or, to put the result briefly if somewhat disrespectfully to the feelings of the learned Academicians, that they had set an absurd subject. Needless to add, the two friends refrained from entering their work for the competition. In their refusal to take Pope seriously as a philosopher, the authors had the support of the poet himself. Speaking of his *Essay on Man,* Pope had written to Swift: "I have only one piece of mercy to beg of you; do not laugh at my gravity, but permit me to wear the beard of a philosopher till I pull it off and make a jest of it myself."

The Lessing-Mendelssohn essay was, however, much more than an exercise in destructive criticism. It was a courageous and a patriotic act. Already in his *Philosophical Dialogues* Mendelssohn had called upon the Germans to throw off the yoke of the French influence in philosophy and he had done so in a manner Lessing himself need not have been ashamed of. "This (French) nation," he says, "which since Malebranche cannot boast of a single metaphysical head saw clearly that thoroughness and profundity were not its strong points. So they concentrated their minds on niceness of manners and they practised their wit and scorn on those who were given to carrying on profound observations and who according to a certain exaggerated standard of refinement did not shine in fashionable society. The few philosophers they still had began to unwrinkle their brows and became pleasing. Finally they even thought in a pleasing manner. They wrote works *pour les dames, à la portée de tout le monde* and they scoffed very wittily at the expense of those gloomy heads whose works contained something more than the fair sex will read. The honest Germans joined them in their scoffing. What else could they do? They would willingly surrender half of their intelligence, if the French would only admit that they had good manners. Will the Germans never recognize their own worth? Will they forever exchange their gold for the tinsel of their neighbours?"

These were strong words to use in Berlin, the centre of the French influence in Germany and right under the very nose of Frederick II who was mainly responsible for the establishment of this influence in his capital. But the unemotional, almost pedantic, demonstration of *Pope, a Metaphysician!* was even more deadly in its effect. It proved beyond a doubt that the highest court of appeal in matters of taste and criticism, the assembly specially selected by Frederick and composed largely of eminent Frenchmen, plainly did not know what it was talking about when it touched on such simple matters as the meaning of poetry and the purpose of philosophy. In the end the consequences to the joint authors were not so unpleasant as they might have been. Neither the booklet nor the authors were burnt by the public hangman on this occasion. While some of the members of the Academy made no secret of their resentment, others showed commendable good sense and declined to take offence. Maupertuis himself, generally so unforgiving, had Mendelssohn solemnly presented to him. Even the court roused itself for a moment from its somnolence regarding works written in German and evinced some curiosity concerning the Jewish youth, "le Juif de Berlin," as he was called, who was not even duly authorized yet to reside in Berlin, but had dared to send the proud Academicians, Frederick's protégés, back to school again.

It is generally assumed that while Mendelssohn supplied some of the ideas, the whole plan of the treatise is Lessing's and that his pen too is responsible for most of the actual writing. Mendelssohn, whose *Philosophical Dialogues* owed a good deal to Lessing's corrections, could not at this time have produced such a masterpiece of polemical style as this joint work proved to be.

For some years Mendelssohn had acted as tutor to the children of Mr. Bernhard, owner of a silk factory. In the course of the year 1754, however, the children passed beyond the school age and Mendelssohn was again faced with the necessity of coming to a decision regarding his future career. He was as far as the boy of fourteen had been from fulfilling the indispensable condition for becoming a moneylender. He was as poor as he had ever been. The profession of rabbi which he was in every way qualified to enter held little charm for him in view of the predominance of the pernicious Polish elements in contemporary Judaism. When Bernhard offered him the post of bookkeeper in his silk factory he felt he had no choice, so he accepted. This occupation, though not particularly enticing to a student of metaphysics, at least held out a promise of moderate comfort, freedom of thought and some leisure for his studies. The work seemed at first hard and was always unspeakably irksome. His letters contain many a pathetic groan on the subject. No doubt he looked upon himself, the bookkeeper by day and the philosopher by night, as no less monstrously incongruous than Pope who had been a poet while alive and of whom the Academicians wanted to make a metaphysician after he was dead.

V

NICOLAI, A PHILOSOPHIC DILETTANTE

An influence akin to that of Lessing now came into Mendelssohn's life through his acquaintance with Christian Friedrich Nicolai, a young Berlin bookseller, who, as the result of a surfeit of pietistic pabulum in early youth, had adopted a most uncompromising form of rationalism. He was largely self-taught. At the age of nineteen his native combativeness found its first victim in Gottsched, the chief prophet of the French literary influence in Germany. There were various bonds of sympathy between Mendelssohn and Nicolai. Both were business men, neither had been to an university and both, making a virtue of necessity, prided themselves on the fact that they were thus able to take a more unprejudiced view of things than most academically trained metaphysicians. They were certainly able to travel with much lighter baggage and progress more rapidly than those "damned professors." While the modest and gentle Mendelssohn contented himself with the quiet enjoyment of this conviction, it developed with Nicolai into openly expressed unbounded contempt and virulent hatred for academic philosophers and all their works. He was no respecter of persons, not even of Kant, the philosophic Olympian, and when the *Critique of Pure Reason* appeared in 1781 it was made the recipient of a particularly venomous vial of wrath. He has been called by Minor [1] "the most wooden-headed representative of the age of utilitarian enlightenment" and he would be a bold person indeed who denied this. Twenty years after the Common Sense Philosophy had been buried in the dead of the night, Nicolai still continued fighting its battles with undiminished fury. He must have reminded the onlookers of the Russian soldiers of whom Frederick tells us that they were too stupid to fall down when they were shot dead and so remained standing. Apart from this obviously incurable vice of woodenheadedness he really formed an admirable link between Lessing and Mendelssohn for while a fellow-feeling of philosophic dilettantism bound him closely to the latter, he had in questions of erudition, for which Mendelssohn always showed but little comprehension, much more in common with Lessing.

If as a writer Nicolai is chiefly a producer of bourgeois platitudes and the cheapest of rationalistic propaganda, he is entitled to a high place in our esteem as an energetic and fearless publisher and editor. Together with Mendelssohn he began the publication of the *Bibliothek der schönen Wissenschaften und der freien Künste* containing not only

[1] J. Minor, Lessing's *Jugendfreunde*.

critical reviews of published works but also original treatises on literature and philosophy. A few years later he started with Lessing, Mendelssohn and Abt the publication of the twenty-four volumes of *Briefe die neueste deutsche Literatur betreffend* (Letters Concerning Recent German Literature) and in 1765, with the cooperation of a great number of contemporary writer, the *Allgemeine deutsche Bibliothek* which lived until 1805. All these periodicals stood originally for independence and freedom of thought and the abolition of cliques and they aimed at the formation of sound critical judgment in Germany. It was only after 1785 when Lessing and Mendelssohn were dead that a process of fossilization set in. Nicolai's freedom of thought which had until then been a cornerstone of the new criticism became the millstone around its neck and Nicolai's name became a synonym for shallowness and aridity. It was his misfortune to live too long. He was less lucky than his friend Lessing who was mercifully spared the bitter mortification of finding his philosophy and some of the aspects of his literary critical method becoming obsolete. The *Critique of Pure Reason* which swept away the Common Sense Philosophy was published the very year of his death and he died before he published an adverse review of *Werthers Leiden* which would have shown him to be out of touch with the modern literary movement just setting in.

It is easy to see that Mendelssohn's intimacy with

Nicolai was not an unmixed blessing for the former. Of the intellectual stimulus to the thinker and the moral support their association afforded the Jews generally in the eyes of the public there can be no doubt. On the other hand, Nicolai only confirmed Mendelssohn in his mischievous common sense attitude towards all philosophical and literary questions and some of the ridicule Nicolai so honestly came by attached itself to the name of Mendelssohn. Lessing, although closely associated with Nicolai and holding similar views in philosophy, was saved from the worst excesses of prostration before the altar of common sense by the possession of profound learning and a due appreciation of the fundamental value of erudition.

VI

MENDELSSOHN AS LESSING'S ALLY

As already mentioned, the three friends cooperated in the publication of the *Letters Concerning Recent German Literature* which more than anything else roused a sleepy and self-satisfied public. They soon assumed such importance that Leipzig and Zürich, which had hitherto been the centres of literary criticism, stepped into the background and Berlin assumed the leadership in matters of literary taste.

The range and variety of Mendelssohn's reading as evidenced by the articles he contributed to these *Letters* and by his correspondence with Lessing and others are all the more astonishing when we take into account the limited leisure enjoyed by Mr. Bernhard's bookkeeper. No less admirable is his refusal from the very first to allow himself to be dazzled by the great names of the day and blinded to the weak spots in their works. Klopstock, the author of the *Messiah,* was at the time the idol of the German public who looked upon all adverse criticism of their poet as downright blasphemy though the irreverent Lessing had already ventured to suggest that "he was probably more admired than read." In Mendelssohn's criticism of Klopstock's *Messiah* and of his dramatic ventures *Abel's Death* and *Solomon* there is no trace of iconoclasm, nothing of the disintegrating, destructive tendency the Jews have so often been credited with; there is no desire even to please Lessing. All he gives is a cool, unbiased judgment founded on plain common sense. The great Klopstock himself, spoilt though he was by praise of incredible fulsomeness, saw the reasonableness of the courageous little Jew's adverse criticism which he took into account in the second edition of one of the plays.

On the other hand, the importance Mendelssohn attached to reason and common sense as the main criteria of artistic excellence occasionally renders his critical attitude wooden and prosaic and he then seems quite incapable of appreciating real flights of imagination and depths of passionate feeling. Thus his common sense, which had enabled him to spot with unfailing certainty the defects of Klopstock's *Messiah,* completely blinded him to the genuine poetic merits of Rousseau's *Nouvelle Héloïse.* It is very characteristic that what Mendelssohn with his ethical preoccupation admires without reserve in *La Nouvelle Héloïse* are the moralizing portions, particularly the letters in which Sir Edward Bomston tries to dissuade St. Preux from committing suicide. Indeed the correspondence between St. Preux and the English nobleman he considers to be the best portion of the whole work. That M. de Wolmar, a virtuous man and of a cheerful temperament, is nevertheless not convinced of the existence of a Deity appears to Mendelssohn quite incomprehensible and constitutes, according to him, a serious anomaly in the portraiture of de Wolmar's character.

Mendelssohn grants that Rousseau writes a language of the most entrancing beauty whenever he has occasion to speak the language of "exalted reason," meaning we may suppose "whenever he moralizes," but he regrets that Rousseau, while he seems to have reflected on the nature of passion, has never felt it himself and is thus unable to speak its genuine language. Some of St. Preux' passionate love-letters which he quotes—and they are by no means the best —impress the normal reader with their sincerity, but they leave Mendelssohn unmoved, they are "affected, bombastic and mere hairsplitting esprit." Perhaps this failure to recognize the language of passion is only to be expected of one whose youth was spent amidst the traditions, though not within the actual walls, of the ghetto where our romantic conception of love played no part if it was not altogether unknown.

Mendelssohn took his duties as a critic very seriously. He shows none of the wild joy with which Lessing rushes into the fray, he approaches his task seemingly after mature consideration and conscious that he has a duty to fulfil not only to the public but also to the author he criticizes. He scolds him gently.

almost paternally. One can almost hear him say:
"It hurts me more than it hurts you." It must be
admitted, though, that, just as in our own youthful
experience, the victim must often have felt hurt out
of proportion to what it cost the chastiser to inflict
the pain. A case in point is his review of a contemporary poetess, Anna Louise Karsch, generally
called *Die Karschin*.

This woman had been born and brought up in very
humble circumstances. She was the daughter of a
country innkeeper. She herded cattle in her early
days and was married twice, first to a weaver and
then to a drunken tailor. Both matrimonial ventures
proved a failure. Though comparatively uneducated
she had always shown remarkable aptitude for composing verse. She rhymed with uncanny facility on
any theme that could be suggested. Then one day
she was "discovered" by a country squire, Baron von
Kottwitz, who took her to Berlin, where she created
a sensation in literary circles. Her poems were published by subscription in 1764 and she received a
record honorarium of 2,000 thalers. The German
Sappho, as she was now called and as she unhesitatingly called herself, maintained her proud position
for a number of years. She met with one great set-
back: she failed to find recognition at Court. She
addressed an ode to Frederick the Great who
acknowledged her homage by sending her two thalers.
Whether this represented in his eyes the value of her

G. E. LESSING

(*Painted by Anton Graff. Engraved by Fried. Müller*)

poetry or whether he meant to be offensive in order to get rid of her is not certain.

With the exception of a good line here and there her verse is commonplace and she had really no better claim to be called a poetess than the lightning calculator of the vaudeville stage has to the title of mathematician. That she should, nevertheless, have been extolled as the equal of all the poets of modern and ancient times shows the desperately low ebb of contemporary literary taste and the need for just such unbiased literary critics as Lessing and Mendelssohn.

In his review of the poems Mendelssohn lays the blame for any unpleasant impression of his criticism on the shoulders of her uncritical friends who have endangered all chance of improvement by persuading her that by mere metrical improvisations she has already reached the pinnacle of poetic excellence. Her friends among whom were to be found Sulzer and Ramler, authorities on the theory and the technique of poetry, ought to have known better than to cultivate in the mind of their protégée, who had read very little herself and possessed no standard of comparison, the idea that the writing of poetry is a mere matter of the inspiration of the moment and requires neither knowledge nor thought, nor strenuous effort of any kind. "As long as these poems," Mendelssohn says, "went from hand to hand in manuscript, considerations of the sex and circumstances of their author might cover up many a fault. But as soon as the reader takes in hand a book in order to read it he will forget who the author is and what his circumstances are. A king, a woman, a Jew, what has this got to do with it? Whoever has the ambition to be an author must be content to be judged as an author and the critic will be all the severer the more he has been promised. This general observation ought to have prevented her friends from giving such a noisy send-off to a work which in many respects stands in need of the indulgence of the reader." Mendelssohn then proceeds to a close and very charitable examination of some of the poems from which the poetess could have learnt infinitely more than from the nauseating flatteries of her friends. In all likelihood neither the poetess nor her friends ever read this excellent criticism if we may judge by the untiring persistence with which the Karschin continued to improvise the same dull, paltry poetry with the same astonishing ease for many years after. Neither Mendelssohn's review nor the strictures of the redoubtable Herder seemed to diminish her popularity. Mediocrity often bears a charmed life.

VII

MENDELSSOHN AS THE CRITIC OF ROYAL POETRY

With what admirable courage and disregard of all personal interest Mendelssohn performed his duty to the readers of the *Letters Concerning Recent German Literature* is shown by the frankness, bordering on rashness, with which he reviewed the *Poésies diverses,* a work by the autocratic Frederick II. Frederick had during his busy life found time to write about twenty-four volumes on history, politics and philosophy and six volumes of verse all published by the Berlin Academy of Sciences. A volume entitled *Poésies diverses* appeared in 1760 and was received by most readers in a manner becoming good and loyal subjects of His Majesty. Not so by Mendelssohn, who distinguished between the aesthetic poetic merit of the king's verse and the philosophic soundness of the ideas expressed. The former he praises; over the latter he gravely shakes his head. Possibly he did not feel competent to set himself up as a judge of French verse, a hard task for a foreigner to undertake anyhow. From his silence on the point we may conclude that he was willing to rest content with the reputation the king enjoyed of writing better French verse than any contemporary German had written. That was probably true enough though, of course, it did not necessarily mean much. He assures his readers, however, that they will rarely find in a poet so much philosophy, such sublime views, knowledge of the human heart, naturalness in descriptions and similes, delicacy of sentiment and, what is the greatest and rarest ornament of a work of genius, the pure language of the heart. "Every verse almost," he says, "is a trait of the character of this prince; the whole is the true portrait wherein his great soul, his even greater heart and even his weaknesses are faithfully delineated."

The eulogistic character of this passage is considerably weakened by what almost amounts to a warning to its readers not to take the praise too seriously. Or is it *par acquit de conscience* that the incorruptible critic prefaces his eulogy with the words: "The tone of the panegyrist is not becoming in the mouth of the subject of a prince. No matter how anxious he may be to adhere to the truth he must after all distrust himself. He must take into account that his heart may have taken sides before the understanding could render judgment." This safeguarding of his critical reputation is followed by a more aggressive attitude which he assumes in the closing sentences of the letter. There he deplores the loss the German language suffers through the prince's greater familiarity with the French. "Were it otherwise," he continues, "our mother-tongue would possess a treasure our neighbours would have good reason to envy us while the illustrious author himself would be spared the humiliation of having to say in his preface:

> Ma Muse tudesque et bizarre,
> Jargonnant un français barbare
> Dit les choses comme elle peut.

All this was mere badinage compared with what followed. After all the appreciation of poetry as such is to a large extent a matter of taste which is proverbially fluctuating and does not lend itself to dogmatizing. Philosophy, on the other hand, raises more serious issues especially with a Mendelssohn who looks upon it as an exact science. Philosophy with him is inseparably connected with natural religion. It is the very foundation of it and of human happiness. That the aim and object of philosophy is the happiness of mankind was in any case at that time a principle so generally accepted that few dared question it. So when Mendelssohn finds the king apparently casting doubt on two fundamental dogmas, the fatherhood of God and the immortality of the soul, he hastens to the rescue of religion and, as he imagines, to the defence of Frederick's reputation. To his *Epître à Maupertuis,* Frederick had prefixed

the motto which is indeed the theme of the poem:
"Providence is not interested in the individual but in
the species." [1] "If this sentence," Mendelssohn
argues, "means that Providence is only interested in
the species and not in the individual it is erroneous,
fundamentally false and unworthy of a Frederick. So
enlightened a head could not possibly harbour such
dishevelled ideas." This being so the King cannot
have meant what he said (in spite of the very emphatic negation "point" used in the French motto!).
He suggests that His Majesty was careless in expressing himself. Had he been less hasty he would
have expressed the idea that was really in his mind
by changing the motto to: "Providence is interested
not so much in the individual as in the species." [2] By
this suggestion Mendelssohn took it upon himself to
correct either the king's philosophy or his French
or both.

Mendelssohn is even more emphatic in maintaining
his belief in the immortality of the soul in opposition
to the view Frederick appears to hold in another
poem, *Epître au maréchal Keith*. The subtitle is
"Imitation of the third book of Lucretius on the fear
of death and the vain terrors of another life." This
to Mendelssohn's great relief seems to justify the assumption that the denial of immortality does not

---

[1] La Providence ne s'intéresse point à l'individu, mais à
l'espèce.
[2] La Providence ne s'intéresse pas tant à l'individu qu'à
l'espèce.

represent the attitude of Frederick but of Lucretius. So without any further inquiry as to what Frederick's convictions really were in this matter he falls foul of the arguments urged by Frederick, arguments "which might have been used in the time of Lucretius, but would cut so sorry a figure in the philosophy of our own time that they scarcely merit an answer." "It seems to me," he concludes, "that a Frederick who does not believe in immortality is a mere chimera, a round square, a square circle." Unfortunately, in spite of this very prettily turned compliment, Frederick really did not believe in immortality.

Now the "roi philosophe" was willing to let any one of his subjects express his opinion quite freely about the Deity and all things divine, but surely a line had to be drawn somewhere and critics must be taught to respect that line. On the battlefield and in the state Frederick had such brilliant achievements to his credit that no carping critic could dim their glory, but in the philosophic field in which he was almost more anxious to shine than in any other, he felt his position far less assured. Even a Frederick is liable to have an inferiority complex and so his gnawing fear of possible inferiority as a philosopher reacted in the usual way; it made him particularly sensitive to criticism in this respect. In showing his dissatisfaction with Mendelssohn's *Letters,* Frederick cannot be said to have acted without provocation. This little Jew, who could hardly be said to have attained the status of a legal person in Prussia and whose cooperation in publishing *Pope, a Metaphysician!* constituted something very like a police record against him in the eyes of the Berlin Academy of Sciences, had told the king that his ideas were dishevelled, erroneous and fundamentally false, his arguments obsolete and not worth answering, that he did not mean what he said and that if he denied the immortality of the soul he gave him the choice of feeling like a round square or like a square circle.

VIII

THE ROYAL POET AND HIS JEWISH CRITIC

The immediate consequences to Mendelssohn were not very serious. The offensive *Letter* was confiscated and the writer summoned to appear before the Attorney-General. He seems, however, to have produced so favourable an impression by his candour and his ready wit that further action against him was dropped. Soon after, the ban on the *Letter* was removed and Frederick's subjects were again at liberty to read what a Jew thought of His Majesty's philosophy and, incidentally, what His Majesty thought of some of the fundamental dogmas of the Prussian state religion.

It is not certain what the summons referred to above really amounted to. According to one version Mendelssohn appeared before the Attorney-General with two charges against him: that in his brazen criticism of the *Poésies diverses* he had been wanting in the respect due to the King's person, and that in an essay directed against the court-preacher Cramer he had shown disrespect to the Deity of the Christian religion. According to another version he had to appear before the King at Sans Souci who may safely be supposed to have shown a livelier interest in the disparagement of his philosophy than in the ruffled feelings of his court-preacher. There is also a report that at a later date Frederick read Mendelssohn's criticism of his philosophy in a French translation made by Signor Venino, an Italian merchant, and that he did so with great satisfaction. Unfortunately the report omits to tell us what exactly it was that could have caused the satisfaction.

The many anecdotes telling of friendly relations between Frederick and Mendelssohn are pure myths. It is doubtful whether Frederick ever quite forgave Mendelssohn though nothing certain is known as to the precise motives of some of the King's subsequent dealings with him. We may, however, confidently assume that matters were aggravated by the fact that Mendelssohn was a Jew and that Frederick with all his display of liberalism was on the Jewish question no more enlightened than the humblest drill sergeant in his army. Soon Mendelssohn was to receive ample proof of this.

The threat of expulsion held out by the Attorney-General as a punishment for disrespect shown to the Christian Deity and the King brought home to Mendelssohn the necessity of acquiring the legal status which would obviate this danger in future. Hitherto he had been merely tolerated as a servant of a privileged Jew or "Schutzjude," but his status was really no better than that of the domestic cat which is allowed to live in peace only as long as it is owned by somebody as a kind of "Schutzkatze" and becomes an outlaw as soon as its owner repudiates it. So he applied to the King for the privilege of residence. "Since the days of my boyhood," he says in his petition, "I have lived in Your Majesty's dominions and I desire to settle therein permanently. As I am foreign born and do not possess the fortune required by law, I take the liberty of petitioning humbly that Your Majesty may graciously condescend to grant me and my children Your Majesty's most gracious protection along with the liberties enjoyed by Your Majesty's subjects in consideration of the fact that I make up for my want of fortune by my endeavours in the sciences which enjoy Your Majesty's protection." No less a person than the Marquis d'Argens, one of the King's favourites, presented the petition. Frederick took no notice of it. D'Argens was not to be put off; his credit as a courtier was at stake. When months later he called Frederick to account, the latter pleaded a misunderstanding and it was only after a second petition had been presented that the request was granted with the minimum of good grace. The privilege of residence was to be purely personal; it could not be transferred to his children and nothing could move the King to change his mind. The only alteration he consented to was that a year later he remitted the fee—it was almost a fine—of a thousand thalers exacted from Jews for the privilege.

Frederick's attitude towards Mendelssohn was no more generous when the Academy elected the Jewish philosopher a member of the institution in 1771. His name had been proposed several times before his friends were successful. The academician Sulzer communicated the Academy's wish to Mendelssohn, adding that if he was willing to accept the honour, the proposal would be laid before the King without delay. Again the King seemed in no hurry to reply. At last the answer came. Mendelssohn's name was crossed off the list of candidates and the academicians were requested to be in future more careful in making their proposals. A new list was drawn up on which the staunch academicians had again placed the name of Mendelssohn. The result was precisely the same and again no reason was given.

From the categorical wording of the first refusal we may draw the conclusion that this refusal was based mainly on a principle which was unconnected with any question of distinction or merit possessed by the candidate, namely, the King's strong dislike of the Jews. He hated all positive dogmatic religions including Christianity, all systems of belief exacting an unconditional submission to dogmas which he considered as, at best, very doubtful. He saw in Judaism the prototype of religious dogmatism, the very name "the Chosen People" was in itself a dogma which nothing in his experience or the history of the Jews in his state seemed to justify. Besides, ever since they settled in the country the Jews had been a nuisance, the cause of unceasing complaints on the part of their jealous Christian rivals in trade and of a bigoted Christian clergy. This necessitated special restrictive and protective legislation which in the end satisfied neither Jew nor Gentile. It meant the recognition by the state of a class of people who refused to be assimilated and whom, as long as they called themselves a nation and clung to their national ideal of a return to Palestine, it was difficult to regard as Prussians in the only sense of the word acceptable to a Prussian sovereign. The Jewish capacity for manifesting patriotism, the Prussian virtue *par excellence,* had hitherto been severely handicapped. When its object was Palestine it was apt to be somewhat ethereal and dreamlike and certainly was afforded few opportunities to manifest itself in action. When its object was the country in which the Jew lived, the feeling was as a rule energetically discouraged as bordering on presumption by the natives in whose eyes the Jew was an undesirable alien and as downright impiety by the orthodox Jews whose one desire was to remain Jews and who naturally looked upon all extra-Palestinian patriotism as a menace to the very existence of Judaism.

Possibly, too, the inevitable conflict in Frederick's heart between his dislike and treatment of the Jews and the precepts of his humanitarian philosophy may account to some extent for the harshness he showed occasionally. In all probability, however, his attitude to Mendelssohn was, on the whole, determined by general public, rather than personal, reasons. In any case we experience some difficulty in attributing it to any vexation Mendelssohn's criticism may have caused him ten years before. It would argue a pettiness we should hardly look for in Frederick the Great.

IX

MARRIAGE

About the time of the publication of his criticism of the royal poems, in April 1761, Mendelssohn went to Hamburg where he met his future wife, Fromet Guggenheim.

He was now in his thirty-second year and he was beginning to tire of his solitude. A Jewish bachelor is an anomaly. Only the head of a Jewish household can be said to live the Jewish life in all its ceremonial fulness. The most joyous religious festivals like the Passover, Purim, Chanukkah, the Feast of Tabernacles, the New Year, indeed every Sabbath day are family festivals or at least partly celebrated in the family circle and presided over by the head of the household. The unmarried Jew of marriageable age and not living with his family has on these occasions neither duties nor privileges; he is the stranger within the gates, welcome but superfluous. Mendelssohn confesses to Lessing [1] that during the week of the Passover celebrations he could not help being cross and out of humour. With his affectionate and

[1] *Works,* V. 89.

deeply religious disposition he felt his loneliness and his position within the community keenly. With the Jews, marriage is not merely a wildly exciting gamble, it is a duty.

The learned Mendelssohn seems to have had a number of opportunities to marry rich Berlin Jewesses in spite of his unattractive exterior, but he preferred, as he writes to a friend [2] many years later, to disregard everything else and to enter the union which best agreed with his inclinations.

On his return from Hamburg he wrote to Lessing as follows: "I should not have been silent so long had I not been to Hamburg where I got entangled in all kinds of distractions. I have been to the theatre, have made the acquaintance of men of learning and, a thing that will surprise you, I have committed the folly of falling in love in my thirtieth year.[3] You are laughing? never mind! Who knows what may happen to you? Perhaps the thirtieth year is the most dangerous and you have not yet attained that.[4] The young woman I intend to marry has neither fortune, nor beauty, nor learning and yet, enamoured fool that I am, I am so captivated by her that I believe I can live happily with her. You will however have a whole year to write the epithalamium." The remainder of the fairly long letter addressed to his most intimate friend deals with Rousseau's *Nouvelle Héloïse,*

[2] *Works,* V. 678.
[3] "Thirty-second year" would have been more correct.
[4] Lessing was at the time in his thirty-third year.

Lichtwer's *Fables,* Burke's *On the Sublime and the Beautiful* but there is no further reference to the theme which we might have expected would monopolize his thought. The few letters he wrote to his betrothed that have come down to us confirm our suspicion that his union was founded on mutual esteem tempered by an affection not far removed from mere friendship. There is not a trace of passion. In July 1761 he wrote to Fromet: "Dearest Fromet, In your father's letter I have made a discovery which pleased me not a little. The kind man assures me that his daughter Fromet is as fair as she is virtuous. What do you think? May we take the honest man's word for it? This good Mr. Abraham Guggenheim must surely know that even philosophers are fond of beautiful things. Yet I beg his pardon. I know his Fromet better than he. She is fair, but she is not as fair as she is virtuous, not as fair as she is affectionate. I envy you, dearest Fromet, your felicitous way of expressing your gentle affection. Your shortest letters are full of affection, full of feeling. The language of the heart is your natural language, and your generous principles take the place of that chilly wit which disfigures the letters of others. Continue, dearest and most affectionate Fromet, to give me the pleasure of your amiable letters. I find it almost impossible to miss a single post or to be happy when an expected letter does not come. What is man when he is not happy? As long as we have to be separated, we must not miss an opportunity to think of one another. It gives me no little pleasure when I can think: now Fromet reads my letters, now Fromet writes to me, now she is vexed because she is disturbed and now she is happy because she has found the right expression." While the lover is not altogether silent in the letter just quoted, the dominant note is rather the paternal and the references to Fromet's letters remind the reader of the literary preoccupations of Mendelssohn, the reviewer.

After an engagement lasting a year Mendelssohn brought home his bride. It took him all this time to make arrangements that would provide for the increased expenditure of the future. He made a satisfactory contract with his employer which not only assured him of a permanent position and a satisfactory income but also of the leisure he needed for his literary work. He now had a home such as he had never had in his life. Fromet proved an admirable wife for whom his love increased rather than diminished as time went on in spite of her obvious mental insignificance. We have a letter he wrote to his friend Abt some weeks after the wedding. It shows us Mendelssohn on his honeymoon gently tormented by his conscience for wasting his time in making love. "For some weeks past I have neither spoken nor written to a friend, I have neither thought nor read nor written anything. I have only been dallying, feasting, observing sacred ceremonies and I have been obliged to be on exhibition now here, now there, and to spend my time on a thousand important trifles. . . . A blue-eyed girl whom I now call my wife has dissolved the chilly heart of your friend into feelings and has entangled his mind in a thousand distractions from which it now seeks to disentangle itself gradually." A year later he began already to groan under the load of his responsibilities, the labour they entailed and the lack of inspiration in the life he was leading. "According to my way of thinking," he wrote to Lessing, "I am happily married and I cannot complain of the way I am situated. But my office work, my tiresome office work, depresses me and devours the strength of my best years. Like a beast of burden I crawl heavily laden through life and, unfortunately, my vanity often whispers in my ear that nature intended me perhaps to be a racehorse. What can we do about it, my dear friend? We will pity each other and be contented. As long as our love of the sciences does not grow cold, we may still hope. Hasten back to me, my friend. Your society alone can give me back the enthusiasm I have lost, can raise my thoughts to a level worthy of my destiny. You cannot imagine how insipid all society has become, since I have to do without yours."

X

MENDELSSOHN WINS THE PRIZE OF THE BERLIN ACADEMY

It speaks volumes for Mendelssohn's mental energy and particularly his powers of concentration that during the very year which tended rather to decentralize his interests and to diminish the leisure requisite for philosophic thought, during the period beginning with his wedding and ending with the pathetic groans he transmitted to Lessing, he should have found it possible to compose a work of the solidity of the essay *On Evidence in the Metaphysical Sciences* (Über die Evidenz in den Metaphysischen Wissenschaften). A prize of fifty ducats for an essay on this subject had been offered by the Berlin Academy for the year 1763. The specific question to be investigated was whether metaphysical truth could be demonstrated by evidence as convincing as mathematical truth. As set forth in his preface Mendelssohn undertakes to show in his essay that the most important metaphysical truths can by an unbroken chain of argumentation be reduced to principles which by their very nature are as undeniable as the axioms of geometry, but that this chain of arguments cannot be presented as clearly and intelligibly as mathematical truths. He anticipates and parries the smile of the jeering sceptic by pointing out that the principles of differential calculus, too, are just as undeniable as geometric truths but that they are not so lucid and intelligible and that we cannot, therefore, ascribe to them the strength of evidence of geometric truth. In the essay he seeks to prove his thesis by examining the principles first of Mathematics, then of Metaphysics, Natural Religion and Ethics. The modern reader will probably discover that some of the metaphysical truths set forth in them are far from being demonstrated with the certainty of mathematical truths. The existence of a Deity as a postulate of reason and not merely of our moral consciousness is hardly tenable since the time of Kant's *Critique of Pure Reason* and the principles of ethics have in our time assumed a complexity of appearance which refuses to be reduced to the naïve simplicity of Mendelssohn's time. Underlying a good deal of Mendelssohn's argumentation there seems to be the vitiating principle that the clearness of our idea of a thing is a proof of its objective existence, a principle by no means dead in our own time.

The Academy's prize was awarded to Mendelssohn, a victory all the more remarkable as Immanuel Kant, at that time an obscure lecturer at the University of Königsberg, came second. Although Kant's essay is generally considered to be superior to Mendelssohn's with regard to method and results, the Academy can hardly be blamed for their decision. Kant's method and perhaps also his language were in sharp contrast to the extraordinary charm and transparent clearness of the language of Mendelssohn, the warmth of his obvious personal interest and conviction and the popular mode of treatment. All this won the hearts of the very human Academicians. As half the members of the Academy were French, Mendelssohn benefited by a fact he had so patriotically deplored in his *Philosophic Dialogues,* namely, that in philosophy the French laid greater stress on elegance of expression than on depth of thought.

When we consider its results the Academy's error of judgment was far from regrettable. It set the seal of its approval and commendation on what amounted to nothing less than a reform in the language of philosophy. The use of German in place of Latin in philosophical treatises was still something of an innovation. The language had still to be created. The first attempts had been crude and the profundity of the thoughts of the philosopher was often made unfathomable by the clumsiness and the obscurity of the language which came to be considered the necessary concomitants of philosophic thinking. Mendelssohn's example showed the falsity of this idea. He showed the possibility of being profound without becoming unintelligible, of going to the very root of things without plunging even his cultured readers into a fog.

Moreover, the announcement in the *Berliner Zeitung* of the 4th of June 1763, that the Academy had awarded the prize to the Jew, Moses Mendelssohn, marks the beginning of a new era in the relations between Jews and Christians. The public recognition of not only the equality but the preeminence of a Jew seemed to cast a new light on the possibilities of what had hitherto been known only as a despised race of pedlars and moneylenders. Clearly also the spiritual emancipation of the Jews had come out into the open; indeed so far as the Jews of Berlin were concerned it was an accomplished fact. The walls of the spiritual ghetto had crumbled with astonishing rapidity. When Mendelssohn came to Berlin in 1743 the Jews punished the mere possession of a German book with expulsion. Now they were ready to honour a Jew who not only possessed German books but wrote them. Even before the Academy had made their award the Jewish congregation of Berlin resolved that in recognition of his great services, especially in composing and translating the sermon preached and the hymns sung on the occasion of the peace celebrations, Mendelssohn was to be free for all time from congregational dues and taxes. Nine years later the question of services rendered to the Jews in particular is entirely left out of consideration and the same congregation honours him "as a distinguished man who being as such above all statutes and regulations could be elected to any office in the congregation without having to observe the prescribed routine of gradation and other limitations."

XI

PHAEDO

Mendelssohn had not yet climbed to the pinnacle of his fame. Few people read his prize essay which the Academy published in a Latin and a French translation together with Kant's essay. The subject hardly appealed to the general reader. He himself felt by no means as elated as one might have expected. To his friend Abt, who had at one time thought of competing for the prize, he wrote with characteristic modesty: "Do not believe that I imagine that I have carried off a victory because the Academy awarded me the prize. I know only too well that in war it is often the inferior general that proves victorious." What doubt, however, there still might have been in his mind or in the minds of others as to the place that was his due among contemporary philosophers was removed by the publication of his great work on the immortality of the soul, his *Phaedo*.

The question of the immortality of the soul was one of the burning questions of the day. The rationalistic philosophy of the Enlightenment had caused such devastation in the theological field of revealed religion that the total annihilation of all religion seemed to be in sight, indeed had already been brought about in the materialistic systems of some of the French philosophers. Most of the German and Scottish philosophers, on the other hand, along with the great mass of the educated portion of the public, clung to the belief in the existence of God and the immortality of the soul. These beliefs they delivered from their condition of theological servitude by maintaining that, as they could be demonstrated with the help of reason, there was no need of revelation with regard to them, that, therefore, they properly belonged to philosophy and not to theology.

Most of these philosophical demonstrations were illogical, some were positively childish. It was claimed that the annihilation of the soul would amount to a repudiation of the plan of creation if the perfections acquired more or less by all men during this life were to vanish entirely; that man feels within himself an unsatisfied desire for happiness which is in itself a guarantee of a happy existence beyond the grave; that man's unsatisfied sense of justice requires another life in which justice will be done. Some realized the difficulty of imagining the soul as perceiving, feeling and thinking when separated from the organs of the body. Few had the admirable frankness and good sense of the psychologist Schwab who admitted that his belief in immortality was based entirely on feeling and added: "This is no demonstration, but it is not meant to be one, for I cannot consider it advantageous to truth when we try to demonstrate where demonstration is impossible." The fundamental error underlying all these "demonstrations," an error which almost precluded the possibility of an unsatisfactory negative result, lay in the fact that most of these philosophers set out to prove what they strongly wished to be true. It may be assumed that a theological bias, acquired in early youth and from which few found it possible to free themselves completely, still further shackled the investigator.

Now, though Mendelssohn was no doubt similarly handicapped he yet made the most serious attempt of his time to consider the problem along strictly scientific lines. For a long time the topic had occupied his mind. As early as 1760 he had resolved that if he could only give up the irksome reviewing for the *Letters* he would tackle the work of partly translating and partly rewriting Plato's *Phaedo* in the light of modern psychology. In 1764 a correspondence into which he had entered with his friend Abt on the subject of the destiny of man and immortality gave him an opportunity of setting out his thoughts and musings with some regard to logical sequence and method. He proposed to his friend that they should assume the names of two Greek philosophers. This should not tie them down to any particular system. The object was merely that they should be able to express their boldest doubts which they might often hesitate to acknowledge as their own and set them down to the account of a defunct philosopher. Two years later referring to his *Phaedo* now seriously taken in hand he tells Abt that he is putting all his arguments in the mouth of Socrates. "I run the risk," he says, "of making a Leibnitzian of Socrates. That does not matter. I need a pagan so as not to have to refer to revelation." It is clear that he at least intended to steer clear of theological preconceptions. We shall see with what success.

Phaedo, or on the Immortality of the Soul (Phaedon oder über die Unsterblichkeit der Seele) appeared in 1767. It consists of an introductory sketch of the life and character of Socrates and three dialogues. The life of Socrates as given by Mendelssohn makes us feel that the author's fear that in his hands Socrates might become a Leibnitzian has been fully justified. We could hardly expect a Greek Socrates from Mendelssohn who was quite incapable of imagining and studying a character of the past in the cultural environment to which he belonged and apart from which he becomes meaningless. He utterly lacked all historic sense and his knowledge of history was of the slenderest. "I yawn every time," he says in 1765, "that I have to read anything historical unless the style enlivens the writing." Although a year later he had come to the conclusion that it was really indecent to be so ignorant of history and he asked a friend's advice as to what he should read to regain his self-respect we can have little faith in the efficacy of the conversion manifesting itself by the time he published the *Phaedo* a year later. Ignorant of the cultural and social conditions of ancient Greece he had perforce to place his victim in the only environment he knew, that of his own time. So Socrates became an eighteenth century Enlightenment philosopher of a strongly marked bourgeois hue and when Mendelssohn's admirers called Mendelssohn the modern Socrates this was true to this extent that the central figure of this modern *Phaedo* was indeed none other than Mendelssohn himself.

As the result of this transformation a great deal of what we are accustomed to associate with the historical Socrates has to be explained away or whittled down. The passionate friendship of Socrates for Alcibiades, as portrayed by Plato, is called "unnatural gallantry to be excused only by the fact that such passionate language was at the time the fashion just as even the most serious man of our own day would not hesitate when writing to a woman to talk amorously." "Plato's expressions," he adds, "mean nothing more, however strange they may sound in our ears." What Socrates called his *daimon,* a warning voice within him, was also more than an Enlightenment philosopher with his contempt for the superstitions of the past could be expected to accept without a reproving frown. This *daimon* is explained as probably something of a pathological character, a weakness. "Must an excellent man," he asks, "be necessarily free from weakness or prejudice?" He even suggests that Socrates really did not hold this belief in the *daimon* but did not consider it worth his while to combat this deep-rooted superstition of the time. These are only a few instances that show that as the result of all this trimming and filing there remained little of the original Socrates beyond the name. Kanngiesser [1] is not far wrong when he calls Mendelssohn's Socrates "a model of triviality and insipidity." In philosophic method, too, this Socrates does not deny his origin. We see the same foolish attempts to make everything clear to the man in the street, no matter how abstruse the subject under discussion; the same set purpose to combine truth and edification resulting too often in the sacrifice of truth to edification; the same endeavour to relate metaphysical truth to conduct and to neglect truth that cannot be so related.

Other writers had in the eighteenth century assumed more or less transparent disguises as a measure of safety to be able to speak their minds more freely. Montesquieu mercilessly satirizes the political, social and literary conditions in France in his *Lettres Persanes,* masquerading as a Persian visiting Paris. The practice was very common about that time and it misled nobody. But by prefixing a would-be historical account to the dialogues Mendels-

[1] G. Kanngiesser, *Die Stellung Mendelssohns in der Geschichte der Aesthetik.*

sohn appeared to invest the Socrates of the dialogues with an air of authenticity he was far from deserving, and the result is irritating.

In the first of the three dialogues on the main subject—Immortality—he seeks to show that the process of nature is a constant uninterrupted change. In this process there is neither cessation nor sudden transition. So gradual is the change that there cannot be two states of a thing between which there is not a third. Now if the soul is to die it must die either suddenly or gradually. It cannot die suddenly because this would be a sudden transition from being to not-being and between these two there is such a terrible chasm that the gradually working nature of things cannot get over it. Even if the soul died gradually, no matter by what infinitesimally small changes, it must sooner or later come to the point where the terrible chasm between being and not-being will have to be crossed. The possibility of this happening by the direct interference of the only worker of miracles, God, is eliminated by what is, of course, a gratuitous assumption, that the all-good Creator and Preserver of thii.gs could not destroy His miraculous work.

That the above proof applies not only to the indestructibility of the soul but that of all things, animate and inanimate, was obvious. So in the second dialogue he seeks to demonstrate that the soul differs from all other things by being a simple substance independent of the compound bodily organism. The simplicity of a substance precludes the possibility of its being broken up into component parts and therefore of its destruction.

The third dialogue is pure theology. In the first two dialogues Mendelssohn thinks with his head, in the third with his heart. When the question is raised what guarantee we have that on the death of the physical organism the soul, while, of course, remaining indestructible, does not subside into a sleeplike state such as we know from our experience of sleep, giddiness and fainting fits, the answer is that it cannot possibly be in accord with the plan of an all-good Creator that spirits striving after perfection should be pushed back into the abyss or stopped half way in their development. "It would be a contradiction," he says, "of all the attributes of God, His wisdom, His kindness, His justice if He created only for a limited space of time rational beings striving after perfection."

Nothing is so instructive regarding the difference of viewpoint and mentality of different ages as seeing what appealed to any particular age as a perfectly unanswerable statement of a doctrine. When Mendelssohn's *Phaedo* was published it seemed to the great majority of the readers that the great question of the immortality of the soul no longer admitted of any doubt. It was settled for ever. After this, people might as well doubt that twice two make four as doubt the immortality of the soul. Against the alarming materialistic propaganda of French philosophers like Helvétius, d'Holbach and Lamettrie, Mendelssohn's *Phaedo* sounded a clarion call which to many meant both the beginning of the battle and the victorious end. People read it with a feeling of intense relief analogous to that caused by the deliverance from a great national peril.[2] The will to live was again safely enthroned and legitimized beyond cavil. So, of course, was the will to believe. It may be assumed that even if the arguments had been weaker than they really are, the effect of Mendelssohn's eloquent advocacy would have been pretty much the same. Objections were indeed raised by contemporaries but in view of the general readiness to accept the glad news they made no impression. Kant, some years later, swept away the whole of Mendelssohn's argument based on the simplicity of the soul substance in a few paragraphs, barely a couple of pages, which have remained unanswerable to the present day. But as they were tucked away in the Fifth Supplement to the *Critique of Pure Reason* which proved an effective barrage against those who wanted to do their philosophy with their hearts instead of their heads, few probably got as far as the Supplements.

What captivated the reader of the *Phaedo,* apart from the ethical satisfaction obtained, was the style, the clearness and the elegance of expression, the play-

[2] This effect was universal. The *Phaedo* was translated into French, English, Danish, Dutch, Italian, Hungarian, Polish, Russian and Serbian. Kayserling, *Moses Mendelssohn.*

ful ease with which he handles his problem and which
seemed to bring the abstract to the very doorstep of
all who could read. Nor could anyone fail to be impressed by the personal charm and the obvious sincerity of the writer and carried away by the warmth
of his conviction and the joyous fervour of his enthusiasm. The public now forgot all they had ever
said or heard said against the Jews and acquaintance
or correspondence with Mendelssohn became an honour and a mark of distinction. Only the loafers and
the street arabs of Berlin, not having read *Phaedo*
nor probably worrying much about the immortality
of their souls, continued to treat the author according
to approved medieval traditions by pelting him and
his children with stones. For different reasons, a few
of the orthodox Christian theologians also manifested their displeasure. They did so, however, because they had read *Phaedo* and because the idea that
anyone should attempt to demonstrate with the exclusive aid of reason a truth which they claimed we
owed entirely to revelation seemed an encroachment
on the inalienable rights and prerogatives of their
closed profession. It almost amounted to an attack
on revealed religion. That the person who set this
most dangerous precedent was a Jew made the presumption doubly revolting.

XII

LAVATER ASKS FOR TROUBLE

While the whole of Europe was resounding with the praise of the author of *Phaedo,* his very fame involved him in an unpleasant controversy which he would probably have given years of his life to avoid. It was forced upon him by a tactless friend and admirer.

A question was frequently asked when once attention had been drawn to this distinguished and cultured Jew: How can such an enlightened man remain a Jew? On the presumption that every cultured person was bound to be a Christian, the question was sometimes varied to: Why does Mendelssohn not become a Christian? In 1769 this public curiosity found a spokesman in the person of J. C. Lavater, the well-known author of the *Physiognomische Fragmente,* and by profession and mental habits a Protestant minister. He enjoyed during his lifetime a somewhat unenviable reputation as a tactless meddler. Lewes, in his *Life of Goethe,* calls him "a compound of the intolerant priest and the factitious sentimentalist," and Goethe, who had known him intimately for a number of years, regrets in one of his epigrams that nature had seen fit to make only one man of him, since there was ample material to make a worthy man and a rogue. Epigrams are as a rule not inclined to err on the side of charity and so Goethe was probably a little harsh in his judgment. No doubt Lavater was a dangerous mystic cursed with a curiously myopic vision with regard to the feelings of others and the rights of others to their own opinions. On the other hand, there is nothing in his life that suggests the rogue. He was enthusiastic in his friendship, generous in the fervour of his admiration of the merits of others though inclined to be unpleasantly gushing. A man of unflinching courage, who unhesitatingly resisted the tyranny of successive aristocratic and democratic governments of his native Canton of Zürich, he ultimately died a noble death attending the wounded on the occasion of the taking of Zürich by Napoleon's general, Masséna. What led, however, to his undoing in his dealings with Mendelssohn was thoroughly characteristic of this "compound of the intolerant priest and the factitious sentimentalist." His act was a mixture of bigotry, kindness and tactlessness.

Even on the occasion of their first meeting in 1763 Lavater had shown an indecent curiosity regarding Mendelssohn's opinion of Jesus and had done so in spite of Mendelssohn's obvious and very intelligible reluctance to touch upon the subject. In 1769, after the appearance of *Phaedo,* what might on the former

JOHANN KASPAR LAVATER
*(Painted by Heinrich Lips. Portrait in the possession of
Herr Kocher-Lavater, Zürich)*

occasion have been mere indiscretion and want of
manners developed into a morbid solicitude about
the soul of the modern Socrates, a missionary yearning that would not be denied satisfaction. Soon a
mode of approach presented itself. Charles Bonnet, a
well known Swiss naturalist, had towards the end
of a life spent in making discoveries regarding the
breathing of caterpillars, the habits of the tapeworm
and the parthenogenesis of plantlice, made an ex-
cursion into the domain of philosophy and religion.
He called his work *Palingénésie philosophique.* Its
latter part, under the title of *Recherches sur le Chris-
tianisme,* was devoted to an attempt to prove the
truth of Christianity. It was neither better nor worse
than most such attempts, but somehow Lavater
thought the demonstration particularly convincing
and he translated it into German. The printer's ink
was still wet when he sent Mendelssohn a copy of his
*Philosophische Untersuchung über die Beweise des
Christentums* (Philosophic Examination of Christian
Evidences) as the translation was called. It was pref-
aced by the following incredible letter addressed to
Mendelssohn and published along with the text: "I
know your deep insight, your constant love of truth,
your incorruptible impartiality, your loving regard
for philosophy in general and Bonnet's writings in
particular and I shall never forget that gentle modesty with which, in spite of your aloofness from
Christianity, you judged that religion, nor the philo-

sophic esteem which in one of the happiest hours of my life you expressed for the moral character of its founder. All this is so unforgettable and so important that I venture to beg you in the presence of the God of truth, your Creator and Father and mine, to beg and entreat you: not to read this treatise with philosophic impartiality, for I know you will do that in any case, but to *refute the same publicly,* if you can take exception to the more important arguments given in support of Christianity. Should you, however, find these arguments correct I beg you to do what prudence, love of truth and honesty bid you do, what Socrates would have done, if he had read this treatise and found it irrefutable."

In penning the turgid asininities of this epistle nothing was further from Lavater's mind than the idea of the possibility of a refutation. He felt sure of his victory. Mendelssohn was as good as converted and his example would be followed by thousands of his coreligionists. Were any refutation to be attempted Lavater would no doubt act as umpire, Lavater with the conviction riveted to his very bones that Bonnet's arguments were unanswerable and filled to overflowing with the feeling of glorious certainty that the conversion of the author of *Phaedo* was a work particularly pleasing to God. No doubt he meant well, but there is nothing so irritating and embarrassing as a well-meaning fanatical mystic. Mendelssohn found himself in a position analogous

to that of Lessing's Nathan when asked which of the
three religions he considered to be the best. There was
this difference, though, that the guileless Mendelssohn had not a trace of the cunning of Nathan. He
recognized that "his religion, his philosophy and his
civil position provided him with the most urgent reasons for avoiding all religious discussions and to
speak in his public writings of those truths only which
are common to all religions." Obviously any defence
of Judaism was bound to prove directly or indirectly
an attack on Christianity, and while Frederick would
no doubt chuckle over any onslaught on Christianity
made by a Christian or an atheist, an unpleasant situation might arise if a Jew were to attack the state
religion of Prussia. Mendelssohn's unhappiness was
increased tenfold by his deep-seated dislike of
polemics even for his beloved Judaism. "So far as I
am concerned," he says in a letter to Lavater, "Judaism might be overthrown in every polemical text-
book or shown to triumph in every scholastic dis-
quisition, I should never have taken part in the
controversy. Without the faintest protest from me
any scholar conversant or half-conversant with rabbinical Judaism might, with the help of trashy literature which no sensible Jew reads or has even heard
of, give his readers the most ridiculous view of
Judaism. The contempt in which Jews are held I
should like to refute by virtuous conduct and not
by polemical writings."

Nevertheless, in spite of the perils of the situation and his strong disinclination to fight in the public arena, Mendelssohn felt he had no choice. Lavater's outrageously tactless challenge had been a public one and it must be taken up publicly not only in the interest of Judaism, but of truth and public decency. It is at least doubtful if Mendelssohn would have buckled on his armour had he known how widespread the commotion stirred up by his controversy would be and how virulent the passions. The peace negotiations of the Seven Years' War in which the half of Europe had been engaged, said an anonymous writer, had hardly given rise to as much talking or writing as this entirely improbable conversion of a Berlin Jew. The controversy lasted over a year and produced quite a literature mainly due to theological pens.[1] To us the most interesting portion is of course the correspondence between Lavater and Mendelssohn into which Bonnet himself was drawn when he saw that Mendelssohn suspected him of having at least given his consent to the use made of his *Christian Evidences* by Lavater.

Mendelssohn's defence is a most admirable and effective piece of polemical writing, calm and irrefutable. He assures this young counsellor of barely twenty-eight that he has spent many years in an examination of the foundations of his religion, indeed

---

[1] Kayserling gives a number of the titles of French and German contributions, p. 205.

all his studies were undertaken to fit him for this task. "If after an investigation extending over many years the decision had not been entirely to the credit of my religion it would necessarily have been made known by some public act. I cannot see what could possibly have kept me tied to so very severe and so generally despised a religion if in my heart I had not been convinced of its truth. . . . Of the essentials of my religion I feel as firmly, as irrefutably assured as you and M. Bonnet can be of yours and I declare before God that I shall adhere to my principles as long as my whole soul does not change in character. . . . Certain inquiries, however, have to be brought to a finish some time in one's life, if one is to proceed with other things. I may say that with regard to my religion this has been done years ago. I have read, compared, reflected and made my decision." He pleads, in addition that whereas the Jews are entirely excluded from other states (Mendelssohn would not even be allowed to visit his friend Lavater in his native Zürich!) they are enjoying in Prussia a respectable measure of liberty and should therefore be restrained by a feeling of common decency from attacking the religion of the majority of the inhabitants, their protectors.

With regard to Bonnet whom he suspects of complicity in the scheme of conversion, he confesses that he has read many a better defence of Christianity written by English and German writers, more profound and philosophical than Bonnet's attempt. "His conclusions," he says, "seem to follow so little from his premises, that with the reasons he adduces I would undertake to defend no matter what religion. I do not blame the author for this. He may have written for readers who are already convinced as he is himself and only desire to strengthen their faith. When author and reader are agreed on the results to be obtained they will without difficulty agree as to the reasons to be given. But you, dear Sir, certainly astonish me when you look upon this work as sufficient to convert a man who is on principle convinced of the contrary. You cannot possibly have put yourself in the place of a reader who is not already convinced but is to seek conviction in this very work. If, however, you have done this and nevertheless believe that a Socrates would have considered M. Bonnet's reasons irrefutable, then one of us is surely a remarkable instance of the powerful influence of prejudice and education over even those who sincerely seek the truth."

When with the help of this letter reinforced by the freely expressed comments of friends and foes Lavater had fathomed the depths of his prodigious folly he admitted with charming frankness that he had blundered. He apologized most handsomely and unreservedly withdrew his outrageous challenge to Mendelssohn.

XIII

THE "LITTLE SNEAK" BONNET

The whole matter was about to be dropped amidst expressions of mutual esteem, admiration and friendship. Unfortunately M. Bonnet, stung by some passages of Mendelssohn's first letter to Lavater which seemed to disparage unduly the scientific value of his *Evidences* and more particularly to accuse him of plagiarism, insisted on being heard. This necessitated a further exchange of letters written, however, in the friendliest tone. Bonnet's letter begins with a repudiation of Lavater's challenge, an assurance that he had done his utmost to dissuade Lavater from his foolish scheme, one of the reasons given being that the *Evidences* had been written for the exclusive benefit of those of tottering faith within the Christian pale. He was not even addressing himself to the "generals of that army which had become so numerous, who had grown old at their trade, and whose conceit held out no reasonable hope whatever. It was the honest subalterns he was trying to get at whose minds and hearts could still be enlightened and touched." Not for a moment was he thinking of the descendants of "the venerable house of Jacob for whom nevertheless his heart would never cease to offer up the sincerest vows." Somewhat unexpectedly he now begs Mendelssohn to read the *Palingénésie* in toto and in the original French. This would give him a much clearer conception of the idea and the plan of his book. Might he also know who are those English and German writers whose defence of Christianity Mendelssohn considers to be more profound and philosophical, so that he might sit at the feet of these illustrious teachers and study and meditate upon their works? Also as plagiarism has always inspired him with a peculiar feeling of horror he would like Mendelssohn to say exactly what he meant by his statement that "most of Bonnet's hypotheses had originated in Germany." The letter terminates with the offer of his friendship and a request for Mendelssohn's in return.

Mendelssohn's reply was of a kind to smooth Bonnet's ruffled feelings and to allay his suspicions regarding the suggestion of plagiarism but he cannot resist the temptation of indulging in a little controversy on the subject of miracles whereby Bonnet has sought to prove the truth of Christianity. Yielding to this temptation was natural enough in spite of the resolution not to engage in religious controversy. The experience and reflections of the preceding months could not help setting his mind in a controversial groove. We may safely assume that the unpleasant situation created by the Lavater challenge was the

CHARLES BONNET

(*Painted by Juel. Portrait now in the possession of the
Geneva University Library*)

obsession of all the leisure hours his bookkeeping left him and he must often have been toying with the irrefutable things he could say if he only felt at liberty.

Mendelssohn here wisely refrains from attacking Christian miracles in particular, or even the credibility of miracles in any religion, he only denies that they authenticate the mission of the miracle worker. All religions speak of miracles. Are we to deny the credibility of all miracles except those of the religion in which we are born? Why? Moses tells his people that the gift of miracles is no infallible proof of truth and Jesus even more emphatically warns His disciples against the false prophets who will seek to deceive them by great signs and wonders. "Seeing," he says, "that both these lawgivers teach that false prophets too can perform miracles, I do not understand how their successors and apologists can represent miracles as an infallible proof of tradition."

In spite of this controversial note the letter ends with an expression of the warmest gratitude for Bonnet's offer of friendship. "It is with unspeakable joy," he says, "that I accept your friendship which you so generously offer me. It is the most precious gift any mortal can offer me and I cannot without putting your modesty to too severe a test tell you how greatly I am obliged for this magnanimity. If hitherto I have cordially forgiven Herr Lavater the vexation he has caused me I now owe him my sincerest gratitude, for his hastiness has conferred on me the happiness of being allowed to call myself the friend of a Bonnet." The Genevan scientist replied in the same generous tone. He had found a kindred soul in Mendelssohn. "Indeed," he says, "I do not think it would be possible to find in the republic of letters two men more averse to polemics than the modern Phaedo and the author of the *Palingénésie.*"

All this hardly prepared Mendelssohn for the next step taken by Bonnet to manifest his aversion to polemics and his disinclination to enter into controversy with "the venerable house of Jacob for which his heart would never cease to offer up the sincerest prayers." Bonnet published a second edition of his *Evidences.* In the text and notes he controverts the arguments Mendelssohn had advanced in one of his letters. He makes no reference to this correspondence and, therefore, to the source of these arguments, and by unscrupulously predating his edition he gives the reader the impression that Mendelssohn had borrowed his objections from Bonnet's notes [1] in which, moreover, "the venerable house of Jacob" receives precisely that offensive attention which Bonnet had never dreamt of bestowing. Among Mendelssohn's friends this thoroughly disloyal act of the pious apologist aroused the greatest indignation and disgust against the "little sneak" as Lessing calls him. Mendelssohn now decided to follow the advice of his

[1] Mendelssohn, *Schriften,* Vol. III. p. 99.

friends and he set to work on his *Reflections on Bonnet's Palingénésie* (Betrachtungen über Bonnets Palingénésie) which, however, he did not publish for some time. In any case it remained a fragment which would in itself be sufficient reason for delay, but possibly the very frankness with which he states his views accounts for his hesitation.

There is nothing very new in these *Reflections,* nothing that had not been touched upon in his correspondence with Lavater and Bonnet, but the individual arguments are stated so fully and the logical conclusions are drawn so mercilessly that offence might have been given where none was intended. What is of interest is the approach to the problem of the authority of the Christian faith from the Jewish standpoint. Mendelssohn's starting-point is the appearance of God on Mount Sinai in the presence of the whole people. This is not a miracle according to him but an indubitable historical event. On this occasion God not only gave His people certain fundamental laws but he also set His seal on the mission of Moses as the messenger and prophet of God and on any further legislation promulgated by His servant. These laws are binding on the Jews and the Jews only and to lose their validity must be revoked by God Himself in the same solemn authoritative manner in which they were imposed. Add to this the conviction which his reason imposes on him that God has created the whole of mankind for happiness which the Jews can attain only by observance of the law, the non-Jews by merely practicing virtue. The rest is easy. He cannot look upon Jesus as a messenger of God because sometimes explicitly, sometimes tacitly and in an haphazard manner he abolishes Mosaic laws which God gave or authorized to be given after days of solemn preparation and in so impressive a manner. On the other hand, his reason revolts against the Christian dogma which consigns a portion of mankind to everlasting damnation for refusing to believe the unbelievable. "The more closely I examine this extolled religion," he says, "the more my reason is offended. The eternal bliss of mankind is indeed the aim of this religion as of all religions, but on what condition am I offered this happiness? What fetters for my reason!" After a brief synopsis of the Christian dogmas of the Trinity, original sin, incarnation, virgin birth, death on the cross and the Lord's supper he declares: "Before the all-just Judge of the world I hereby testify frankly that I cannot accept any one of these dogmas, that I should have to abjure my reason, if I accepted them as true. They seem to run counter to everything sound reason, unsophisticated reflection, and the sacred Scriptures which we all acknowledge to be divine have taught me. My whole soul would have to be changed if I were to change my conviction. . . . This being so I cannot acknowledge as a divine ambassador the founder of a faith which proclaims such doctrines. I cannot place any reliance on his promises of future happiness since the divine character of his mission would necessarily involve the truth of a doctrine I reject (i. e. that of a salvation by faith). He has confirmed his mission by miracles? What can miracles prove to me? If the founder of this religion in my presence awakened all the dead of past centuries, I should say: the founder of this religion has performed miracles, but I cannot accept his teaching."

At the very beginning of the controversy with Lavater he had inquired of the Berlin Consistory, the ecclesiastical court charged with the function of censorship, how to proceed to obtain the imprimatur of his replies. The answer, which reflects the greatest credit on that body, was that Moses Mendelssohn could have his writings printed without submitting them in part or entire to the Consistory as the members were persuaded of his wisdom and modesty and that they felt assured he would write nothing that would give public offence. We can easily understand that after such a signal mark of confidence he felt a very natural reluctance to print his *Reflections* from which many pious souls would very naturally conclude that Mendelssohn looked upon Jesus as an impostor and a false prophet.

The question has been asked why Mendelssohn was allowed to fight his battles alone, why not a single friendly pen stirred in his behalf and the suggestion has been made that this silence was due to the fact that Mendelssohn was a Jew. "How could anyone dare in so burning a question to express an opinion in favour of a Jew?" asks Kayserling.[2] "The liberal theologians? They were afraid of losing their posts, an imprudent word was as much as their living was worth. They were content to express their high esteem for the courageous champion of his religion in private letters which read like letters of condolence."

The explanation is not very convincing. The Consistory's resolution regarding the censorship of Mendelssohn's defence against Lavater seems to manifest not only a tolerant but even a friendly and sympathetic attitude towards Mendelssohn. In view of this anyone could have publicly protested against Lavater's medieval method of conversion without incurring the Consistory's wrath. Probably Mendelssohn's friends felt that he was quite able to look after himself and was more than a match for Lavater who was so obviously asking for trouble and sure to get it. They were content to watch the fight as spectators. Their only fear was that Mendelssohn might decline to pick up the glove. "Be sure to answer," urged Lessing. "Reply with the greatest possible liberty and all imaginable energy. You alone may and can speak and write in this matter."[3] As

[2] Kayserling, *Mendelssohn.*
[3] Mendelssohn, *Schriften,* Vol. V, 189.

the effect of Mendelssohn's first letter even was to make Lavater withdraw his challenge unreservedly, there was then less need than ever of the help of friends. The result had shown that Mendelssohn could very well be left to fight his battle alone. He had vindicated his right to remain a Jew without interference from people whose missionary zeal blinded them to the claims of ordinary decency and "whose prolonged gazing into eternity had spoilt their eyesight completely for the worldly horizon."

XIV

AN ENLIGHTENED DUKE

The Lavater controversy, however, although terminated so far as the public was concerned, was not to be without its aftermath. The hereditary Prince of Brunswick had read Mendelssohn's *Phaedo* and longed to make the personal acquaintance of the author. His wish was fulfilled on the occasion of a visit to his uncle, Frederick the Great. Mendelssohn was summoned to the palace where the two discussed philosophical and moral subjects and it was agreed that they would correspond about the *Phaedo*. In the meantime Lavater had thrown his missionary bomb and had for the moment turned the Prince's interests in a different direction. So in acknowledging the receipt of a copy of the third edition of *Phaedo* along with a copy of the reply to Lavater, the Prince neglected to make even a formal reference to the subject of *Phaedo*, but urged Mendelssohn to send him his *Reflections* on Bonnet. "Nothing," he said, "could be more important to a man born in the Christian faith than to know how a Jewish philosopher could defend the historical foundations of the Mosaic faith and yet reject those of

Christianity." The harassed philosopher had to confess that these *Reflections* existed at the time more
in his head than on paper but he would accede to His
Highness' request, trusting that his frank confession
would come to the eyes of no one likely to be shocked
by it.

On the whole, his statement of his objections to
Christianity is an epitome of the *Reflections*. He emphatically lays down the principle that he cannot accept any evidence which contradicts a firmly established truth. As the Christian dogmas which he
enumerates flatly contradict all that reason and reflection have taught him regarding the nature of the
Deity he must reject them and if he found such doctrines in the Old Testament he would reject the Old
Testament. Every one of the remarkably clearly and
tersely expressed theses he sets up is a challenge which
carries the war into the camp of the enemy. There is
no longer any thought of standing on the defensive
for Judaism. It is a critical assault on the very
foundations of Christianity. Fortunately the Prince
did not carry out Mendelssohn's request to destroy
a document which shows us the gentle Mendelssohn as a worthy disciple of Lessing with his most
uncompromising pugnacity.

Evidently Mendelssohn's frankness had only increased the Prince's esteem for his correspondent
for in October of the same year (1770) he invited
him to visit him in Brunswick. The invitation proved

a godsend to the tired and worried philosopher.
Fighting brought him no joy and even victory left
him depressed in spirit and weakened in body. Besides, he was beginning to dislike Berlin and even
thought at one time of taking up his residence in the
diminutive town of Bückeburg.

In Brunswick he was received with the greatest
kindness. He spent the whole evening with the Prince
and the Prince's mother, a sister of Frederick the
Great. So great was the Duchess' admiration of her
guest that she hung his portrait directly under that
of her father, Frederick William I.[1] When we remember that it was in the latter's reign that the Jews
were deliberately classed with homicides, blasphemers, murderers, perjurers and adulterers we can ap-
preciate the phenomenal change in the attitude
towards the Jews that had thus been, if not brought
about, at least facilitated by the personality and the
intellectual distinction of one of them.

[1] According to Zimmermann's *Briefe,* quoted by Kayserling.

XV

THE FRAGMENTS, AN UNPLEASANT
SURPRISE

As Wolfenbüttel where Lessing was librarian was at no great distance from Brunswick, it was inevitable that the two friends should meet again. Although only three years had elapsed since their last meeting some of the cheerfulness of former meetings was lacking. Mendelssohn was only beginning to recover from the worries and anxieties of the preceding twelve months and Lessing, too, was anything but happy. As ducal librarian he received so despicable a salary that even as an unmarried man he found it insufficient to satisfy the most modest wants. His employer, Duke Karl, was a desperate spendthrift, very luxurious in his way of living and had, by the time Lessing was appointed librarian, run up a debt of twelve million thalers, which kept him permanently on the verge of bankruptcy. This state of things did not hold out much hope of an improvement in Lessing's finances for many years to come and his marriage with Eva König seemed likely to remain a dream indefinitely.

Mendelssohn was duly impressed by the Library,

but as ill-luck would have it he had come at the wrong
time if he was seeking freedom from the hateful religious controversy. What mainly interested Lessing
at this very period was a manuscript which later became known by the name *Fragments by an Anonymous Writer* (Fragmente eines Ungenannten).

Professor Samuel Reimarus of Hamburg, a Greek
and Hebrew scholar of some note, had in 1768 died
in the odour of unimpeachable piety and orthodoxy.
Yet he had for many years inwardly revolted against
the tyranny and the absurdity of the orthodox religion. For the sake of his family he had kept his
state of mind a dead secret, but had set down the result of his reflections in a bulky manuscript. He called
it *Apology or Defence for the Rational Worshippers
of God* (Apologie oder Schutzschrift für vernünftige
Verehrer Gottes). After his death the family had
entrusted portions only of the *Apology* to Lessing
who after some hesitation published instalments of
the manuscript. Lessing showed it to Mendelssohn and
indeed let him take it away with him to Berlin. Mendelssohn did not share his friend's admiration for the
Fragments. Their frankness shocked him as well it
might. Abraham was made out to be an avaricious
cheat, the sacrifice of Isaac the act of a crazy fanatic
practising the Moloch cult, Moses became the arro-
gant founder of a theocracy without a trace of divine
warrant. Of the Jews as a people the author says that
no nation on earth deserved less to become the Chosen

People as their record was a long series of shameless
and wicked deeds. This relentless method applied to
the foundations of Judaism produced in Mendelssohn
a revulsion of feeling he made no effort to hide. So
great was his concern that before his departure from
Brunswick he mentioned the matter to the Prince
from whom the very existence of the manuscript was
to have been kept secret. On his return to Berlin he
wrote to Lessing on the subject of the manuscript
though he admits he has not yet found time to read
it critically. He holds that the author is bitter and
unfair, that he ought to have taken into account the
remote time when these things happened and the
crude ideas of these times regarding the rights of
other nations and regarding justice and humanity. To
which Lessing replied that the anonymous author
would no doubt have applied this principle to the
characters and acts if he had found them in Herod-
otus, but that he was dealing in this case with patriarchs and prophets who are held up to us as models
of the sublimest virtue and whose most insignificant
acts are represented as indicative of a divine plan.
"The wise man would be doing wrong," he says, "if
he contented himself with excusing things in which
the populace insists upon seeing a divine character,
while we can really hardly excuse them. He must,
on the contrary, speak of them with all the contempt
they may deserve in still better and still more enlightened times. The reason why this procedure has

shocked you in our anonymous author is that you have at all times been less bound to look upon the incriminated acts in a divine light, a view which is imposed upon us." The bitterness of the author is indeed explained by Lessing's contention and by the years of repression during which the anonymous author was compelled outwardly at least to profess a set of views which in his heart he knew to be both absurd and mischievous.

This unwelcome little controversy proved doubly unpleasant. Apart from apparently perpetuating the atmosphere of jarring discord in which a man of his peaceful disposition could scarcely breathe it brought home to him with painful vividness a fact he could hardly fail to be aware of already, namely that in questions of that natural religion which he fondly imagined to be solidly established on a basis of reason there was room for a sharp divergence of opinion. He realized that reason may be used not only to enthrone religion but also to dethrone her and may in any case be enlisted to undermine the foundations of the religion he considered to be the special protégée of reason, Judaism. We may further assume that although the disagreement with Lessing did not bring about a perceptible change in their friendly relations something may have rankled in his mind since that time, a feeling of discomfort, even dismay, that his great mentor and teacher, the best friend the Jews had, should be the very man to broadcast the pestilential *Fragments*. Some time after Lessing's death Mendelssohn wrote that he had never been interested in the matter of Lessing's wranglings (Zänkereien), but only in the characteristic manner and method, indeed he had never read the *Fragments*. Surely an amazing lapse of memory for a Mendelssohn!

XVI

ILLNESS

Mendelssohn had not been back in Berlin many
months when he was afflicted with a serious illness
which showed to what desperate condition his whole
nervous system had been reduced. His sleep became
restless and, on waking up, though he could think
clearly, he was incapable of voluntary movements.
He could neither utter a sound nor open his eyes.
Any effort he made to move a limb, besides being
useless, only intensified the distressing symptoms ac-
companying his condition. He felt as if something
red hot were running down his spine and meeting
with some obstacles or as if someone were lashing
his neck with red hot scourges. In a moment he might
be all right again but writing a page or reading or
even being read to was sure to bring on an attack.
Listening to others discussing philosophy ended in a
fainting fit. He was absolutely forbidden to think.
As he told a friend he would often, when he could
stand this total suspension of intellectual activities
no longer, go to the window and count the tiles of his
neighbour's roof. When two months later he was al-

lowed to spend a few hours daily at his office work he was by no means out of the wood. For some time to come he could not write a letter without feeling dizzy. It was not until a year after that he could put in a full day's work in the factory. A journey to Pyrmont which his physician recommended could not be undertaken in 1772 through lack of means, and was carried out only a year later when a rich coreligionist also bound for Pyrmont offered him a place in his travelling-carriage.

A fortnight in Pyrmont seemed to do wonders and he was overjoyed at the prospect of a complete cure and the possibility of resuming his literary labours, but before long the old alarming symptoms returned and he felt well only as long as he abstained from all writing, reading and thinking. A second trip to Pyrmont became imperative in July 1774. Its results were more lasting than on the first occasion. At least he managed to live through the next few years without a serious breakdown though he was still hampered in his reading and writing by irksome but necessary restrictions. A few years later he was able to satisfy his *Wanderlust* more amply by making a journey to Dresden where he was greeted by many friends. He was both annoyed and amused to find that as a Jew he had to pay the same "entrance fee" as an ox, namely twenty groschen. This sum the authorities paid back with many apologies when they learned on what an illustrious ox the tax had been levied. A year later his firm sent him on business to Königsberg where, as in Dresden, he received the homage of every lover of philosophy and enjoyed the privilege of hearing Kant lecture.

XVII

LAST VISIT TO LESSING

After a stay of six weeks in Hanover where he wellnigh died of boredom he paid a last visit to Lessing. A wonderful change had come over Lessing. He was happy and contented. His finances had been much improved. Most of his debts were paid, he lived in an official residence outside the walls of the depressing castle of Wolfenbüttel, which had at first been his home, and a more liberal salary had permitted him to marry Eva König to whom he had been betrothed for a number of years. During Mendelssohn's visit his cheerfulness and good-humour were proof even against Mendelssohn's somewhat peevish attempt to draw him into a discussion on Freemasonry, a subject in which Lessing, the Mason, was particularly interested at the time. He had just published his *Dialogues on Freemasonry* (Gespräche für Freimaurer) and one of Mendelssohn's letters from Hanover had already warned him that he was unduly exercised over the secrets and mysteries of the craft. When they met at Wolfenbüttel, Mendelssohn expressed his surprise at Lessing's reticence on this subject. After assuring his friend that nothing was further from his mind than trying to worm these secrets out of him, he naïvely adds : "From our earliest youth we have been seeking the truth, ever since we became acquainted we sought her together with all the effort and faithfulness with which she must be sought. Is it possible that there should be truths which Lessing has sworn, solemnly sworn, not to reveal to his friend of twenty-five years standing? Why should I not be curious to know these truths? all the more if what the order reveals to its disciples is not the truth." The more acrimonious Lessing of former years would have taken the greatest delight in getting his overcurious friend entangled in a discussion which would have led nowhere. On this occasion he cut short further inquiries with his heartiest laugh and the two were left to enjoy a day of unclouded happiness, one of the last happy days in Lessing's life. When Mendelssohn returned to Berlin he received the news that Lessing's wife had given birth to a boy, but that mother and child had died soon after.

XVIII

"IS IT SUCH A DISGRACE TO BE
A JEW?"

It would be a great mistake to imagine that because cultured men and women saw in Mendelssohn one of the foremost thinkers in philosophy and aesthetics, because princes honoured him with their friendship and hung his portrait under that of the King of Prussia a golden age of tolerance and freedom from annoyance had set in for the Jews. Far from it. As late as 1780 Mendelssohn could write to a friend: "Here in this so-called tolerant country I am living all the same so hemmed in on all sides by real intolerance that for the sake of my children I have to shut myself up all day in a silk factory as in a convent. Sometimes in the evening I go for a stroll with my wife and my children. 'Father,' asks a child in his innocence, 'what is that boy calling after us? What have we done to them?' 'Yes, father,' says another, 'they always run after us in the street and call us: Jews! Jews! Is it such a disgrace among these people to be a Jew? What can it be to them?'—Alas! I cast down my eyes and I sigh within myself: Oh men, how could you let it come to this?"

In spite of the ungrudging recognition that was bestowed upon individual Jews here and there the civil and social condition of the mass of the Jewish people had not advanced a hair's breadth beyond what it was when Mendelssohn came to Berlin. The law continued to treat the Jews as an inferior race, they were as unwelcome as ever to the common people in whose mind all the basilisks of medieval superstition were lurking. The Enlightenment still left the vast majority of the population in darkness. The only really hopeful symptom of improvement came from the Jews themselves. Slowly at first but soon with ever increasing velocity a reaction had set in against the myopic form of Jewish orthodoxy which saw nothing beyond the world of the Talmud. A certain degree of religious indifference and, as the result, of disintegration no doubt alarmed the die-hards of orthodoxy. This was, however, really so much to the good if the Jews were ever to abandon their attitude of a people set apart for religious and political purposes, indifferent in their hearts to Prussian national ideals, which have also been, like those of the orthodox Jews, of a severely exclusive and uncompromising character.

Mendelssohn himself was far from sanguine regarding the future of the Jews and when in 1770 a correspondent submitted to him a project for the foundation of an independent Jewish kingdom he replied as follows: "The boldness of my spirit, if I have any, extends only to speculative matters. In practical things I have always been confined in too narrow a sphere to acquire the experience that would enable me to rise above the difficulties of everyday life to greater things. Who can add a cubit to his stature?

"The greatest difficulty which stands in the way of the project arises out of the character of my nation which is not sufficiently prepared to undertake anything great.

"The oppression under which we have been living for so many centuries has robbed our spirit of all vigour. This is not our fault. Still we cannot deny that the natural desire for liberty has with us lost its energy. It has changed into a monkish virtue which finds expression in prayer and suffering, but not in action. Considering how dispersed this nation is I cannot even hope for the spirit of union without which the most carefully studied project must fail."

The second half of the letter though not so pertinent to the point at issue is well worth quoting also in view of recent developments in Zionism. "On the other hand," he says, "this undertaking seems to call for enormous sums of money, and I who know that the wealth of my nation consists more in credit than in real possessions cannot imagine that its financial strength is great enough to obtain such sums no matter how much greater their desire for freedom than their love of the shining metal. Even apart from these difficulties such a project seems to me feasible only at a time when the greatest European powers are involved in a general war in which each has to look after itself. But in a time of peace such as they are enjoying at present a single jealous power (and there would be several) could wreck the project. The unfortunate crusades seem to justify this apprehension."

XIX

MENDELSSOHN AS MEDIATOR

In spite of Mendelssohn's aversion to getting mixed up with anything likely to lead to public discussion of his private convictions and in spite of his perhaps overcareful attitude in these matters his distinction and authority were a continual temptation to Jews with a grievance to appeal to him for help. These appeals were very characteristically not concerned with the Jewish situation in general, with the whole system of unbearable oppression, but were provoked by individual instances. As long as they were not threatened with actual expulsion the "monkish virtue" referred to by Mendelssohn enabled them to submit to all the rest of the humiliations their ingenious Christian hosts were unceasingly excogitating.

In 1774 the Governor of Baden in Switzerland decreed that the number of Jews resident in the valley of the Surb was to be kept within certain limits and that consequently a number of persons who had married without the financial guarantees insisted on by the law were to be expelled. In their distress the inhabitants of the district, aware of the friendly relations between Mendelssohn and Lavater, appealed to the former to intercede on their behalf with his friend. Mendelssohn's letter of intercession [1] had the desired effect and as the result of Lavater's mediation the Jews of the Surb valley were left in peace. Mendelssohn was far from going into hysterics over the fate of his Swiss coreligionists. He is careful to admit that he really does not know anything about the circumstances and we can read between the lines that the case interested him only moderately.

The case of the Dresden Jews was of a totally different order. According to a law promulgated in 1772 any Jew who neglected the payment of his personal tax on the appointed day, even though it should be his first offence, was to be expelled. In 1777 hundreds of poor Jews, many of them as the result of unavoidable misfortunes, were to be driven from the city. When appealed to, Mendelssohn was deeply moved by this threat of barbarous injustice and distressed at the thought that the many friends he had at the Prince Elector's court and whose probity and humanity he could not doubt, should allow such a cruel thing to happen. So he addressed the following indignant protest to one of the Prince's councillors, Freiherr von Ferber: "The last post has just brought the news that hundreds of my coreligionists are to be driven out of Dresden. Among

---

[1] Mendelssohn, *Schriften*, III, 106.

these are a number I know personally, of whose honesty I am certain. They have lost their money and are perhaps unable to bear the burdens imposed upon them. I am sure they have come to this not by their own fault, not through prodigality or idleness, but by misfortune. Kind and benevolent father, where are these wretches to go with their innocent wives and children? Where are they to find shelter and protection if the country in which they lost their means expels them? Expulsion is the hardest punishment for a Jew, harder than living in exile, almost equivalent to extermination from God's earth where prejudice turns them back from every frontier by force of arms. And human beings are to suffer this punishment though they are not guilty of any crime, merely because they hold different convictions and have been impoverished by misfortune. How can you expect a Jew to be honest if you punish his poverty as harshly as his dishonesty? I refrain from all further reflections, which might wound the heart of a kind friend. I have hope, well-founded hope, which affords me comfort in the distress of my heart. Under the reign of the best and kindest of princes and the administration of wise and humane men there need be no fear of punishment in the absence of crime. The innocent poor, no matter what their customs and religion, cannot be refused fire, water and shelter. Forgive me, most worthy protector of innocence, if I am not writing to you in the way I ought to. My heart is too full, my mind too agitated and incapable of calm reflection." In this case, too, Mendelssohn's name worked wonders and the iniquitous order of expulsion was withdrawn.

One of the most curious symptoms of Christian distrust of the Jews was the custom in vogue in some parts of Germany of having a government inspector of synagogues. Conscious of the barbarous way in which the Jews had been treated, Christian governments suspected that their victims did not love them, a suspicion that was probably not entirely groundless. To prevent any expression of such possible hostility towards the government or the Christian faith, an inspector, who, of course, had to have a knowledge of Hebrew, acted as watchman for the government and had to report anything of a disrespectful character observed in the service. It proved in most cases a sinecure. Occasionally, however, the inspector's tortuous imagination, assisted by an imperfect knowledge of Hebrew and the will to find, made a fresh discovery or warmed up an old one. A most telling instance is the periodic excitement caused in Europe by one of the most beautiful prayers of the Hebrew liturgy beginning with the word *alenu* meaning: it is incumbent upon us. Hence it is generally referred to as the prayer *Alenu*. One of the passages reads: "Glorify the Creator who hath not made us like the families of the earth. He hath not set our portion with theirs, nor our lot with their multitude, for they prostrate themselves before vanity and folly and pray to a god who cannot help them." As the prayer is of Palestinian origin the reference is obviously to the pagan nations surrounding the Jews in their homeland. Probably owing to the fact that the Jewish martyrs going to their death in the Middle Ages were in the habit of singing this prayer, it assumed a sinister import in the minds of their tormentors. To a baptized Jew, Pesach Peter, belongs the distinction of having been the first to reveal the blasphemous intention of the prayer, in 1399. He maintained that the words "and folly" in the passage quoted above alluded to Jesus "because the Hebrew letters of both words have the same numerical value!" This interpretation, which for sheer abnormal ingenuity rivals some of the arguments used in the Bacon-Shakespeare controversy of our own time, was greedily swallowed for about four hundred years. It was dished up again about the middle of the sixteenth century in a book called *The Belief of the Jews* by Antonius Margarita and shortly after by another irrepressible baptized Jew, a certain Samuel Brenz, who at least showed some originality in the choice of a spicy title for his book which he called *The Jewish Cast-off Snakeskin* (Jüdischer Abgestreifter Schlangenbalg). When the charge of blasphemous intent had been refuted again and again the notorious Eisenmenger

in his *Judaism Unmasked* (Entdecktes Judenthum)
announced the discovery that when reciting the
words "they bow to a god that does not help" the
Jews were in the habit of spitting.[2] These words, he
maintained, accompanied by such manifestation of
contempt, could only refer to Jesus. Though the rabbis saw to it that the practice of spitting wherever it
was found to be in vogue was abolished the Government Inspector Kypke of Königsberg in 1777 made a
report to the authorities complaining of the blasphemous nature of the prayer *Alenu*. An investigation
was ordered to be held and the Jews asked Mendelssohn to give an expert opinion on the origin and
meaning of the prayer. In a clear and dispassion-
ate statement which was transmitted to the authorities he gives the most cogent reasons for the view
that the prayer *Alenu* is not an attack on the Christian faith. It was composed during the time of the
second temple when the extermination of pagan
idolatry was still the chief item in the political and
religious policy of the Jews. The Jews were still in-
habiting their own country and there is no mention
of the destruction of the temple. Considering the awe
with which the Jews looked upon their principal
prayers it is absolutely inconceivable that even the
slightest alteration should have been introduced in

[2] Curiously enough in the early Christian Church, too, converts
had, before being baptized, to accompany the renunciation of
Satan by spitting as a sign of contempt.

later times. This holds good particularly with regard to the prayer *Alenu* the words and syllables of which had been counted and scrupulously noted at an early period. It is found with exactly the same wording among Jews all over the world, not only in Christian but in Mohamedan surroundings in which the Jew was not even remotely interested in Christianity.

Mendelssohn's defence was so clear and irrefutable that the authorities were convinced of the groundlessness of the charge of blasphemy. A further result was that Frederick the Great in answer to a petition presented by the Jews and in spite of Professor Kypke's protest abolished the offensive inspectorship altogether.

Not on every question could the Jews expect an answer favourable to their own point of view. The mere possibility of giving offence never made Mendelssohn hesitate in doing or saying unpopular things where he found his reason at war with mere Jewish prejudice. In 1772 the Duke of Mecklenburg decided that the pernicious Jewish custom of an immediate burial of their dead should be made illegal on account of the danger of people being buried alive. The Jews of the Dukedom vehemently protested against what was really according to them an order to break and abrogate a Mosaic law, an act which would surely draw down on them the wrath of God. Only one man could champion their sacred cause, Mendelssohn, who was petitioned to draw up a memorial on the question which would demonstrate to the authorities the heinousness of the new regulation. Mendelssohn did nothing of the kind, instead of cursing the ducal decree, he blessed it. He asked his petitioners how they could possibly all be up in the air about so very salutary a law. Early burial was a practice and nothing more. There was no Mosaic law on this matter and even if there were, he reminds them, it was a fundamental principle of their religion that no law was valid where its application involved danger to life. He asked them not to expect any great result from the memorial he was sending them just to please them.

The upshot was as Mendelssohn expected, that the Duke declined to budge and that the Jews submitted. They were not visited by the wrath of God, but Mendelssohn was involved in a disagreeable correspondence with one of the protagonists of the old school, Jakob Emden or Hirschel, who had also been asked by the distressed Mecklenburg Jews to give an opinion. Having given it strongly in support of the old Jewish custom he took Mendelssohn to task for what he considered to be a deviation from the straight path of the true faith. When Mendelssohn proved recalcitrant he accused him of pride and arrogance and advised him for his own sake to avoid all suspicion of unbelief. He was, he added, already being blamed for "bringing up a vicious dog in his house," i. e. for studying philosophy, and frequenting the society of men of loose religious principles.[3]

[3] Kayserling, *Moses Mendelssohn*, "Ungedrucktes und Unbekanntes."

XX

A LUDICROUS FORM OF PERSECUTION

If hitherto Mendelssohn's voice had made itself heard with no uncertain sound and without fear or favour in the cause of reason and justice we shall find his attitude on the question of the Jewish oath puzzling if not positively embarrassing. On the assumption that Jews in a Christian court of law imagined themselves to be exempt from speaking the truth the oath taken by a Jew was hedged about with ceremonies, admonitions and a phraseology intended to have a terrifying effect. Even in Mendelssohn's time the following procedure was prescribed by law.[1] Whenever a Jew's evidence was called for he had to take his oath in the synagogue, if possible on a Monday or a Thursday, in the presence of an officer of the court and of ten adult Jews, one of them a rabbi. The person about to be sworn had first to wash his hands, put on praying-shawl and phylacteries, take in his hand the scroll of the law and place his arm over Exodus chap. 20, v. 7. Whenever the oath was of particular importance he had to don grave-clothes and holding a butcher's knife

---

[1] Geiger, *Geschichte der Juden in Berlin.*

in his hand sit on a coffin. Before the oath was taken he had to be reminded by a rabbi of the seriousness of the oath and of the right a Christian court had to require him to speak the truth. In a lengthy formula he had to invoke God to load him with curses in case he failed to speak the truth. "If I do not speak the truth," he had to say, "I shall not expect forgiveness from God nor reconciliation on the Day of Atonement in this world or the next. No repentance shall avail me and God shall send down upon me all the curses of Balaam and all the ten plagues of Egypt. He shall punish my house and my chattels, my wife and my children with fire and brimstone as he punished Sodom and Gomorrah. Let me be Orur and Cherem, banished and cursed and may body and soul have no part in all the promises made by God."

In 1760 a change was made by the government. The new version exempted at least the family from the fire and brimstone and the oath could be taken either in court or in the synagogue at the discretion of the judge. At the suggestion of one of the Jews consulted by the government the preliminary admonition was rendered from German into the most unspeakable jargon.[2] It is on this jargon and not on

---

[2] The opening paragraph reads as follows: Unter allen Mitzwos lo saace, welche den Menschen, wenn er sie tut, um chelek olam hasah und chelek olam habo bringen können, ist die Avero von schebuos schavooschecker die grösseste, weil sie allein so gross ist, als avodo soro, gilluy arajos und schephichos domim, wie Rambam in Parschas Jisro beweiset.

the offensive implication of the whole oath that Mendelssohn concentrated his efforts when in 1782 Klein, a judge, charged with an inquiry into the question of the oath among other things invited his cooperation. Mendelssohn's main contention was that the admonition should be either in pure Hebrew or in pure German and he proposed a German version which was adopted. "I am unwilling to see," he said, "the Jewish-German dialect and the mixture of Hebrew and German authorized by the government. I am afraid that this jargon has contributed not a little to the immorality (*Unsittlichkeit*) of the common man and I expect good results from the ever increasing use of pure German among my brethren. How vexed I should be if the law of the land encouraged the misuse of both languages." As to the offensive oath itself it remained very much as it was and it continued to be an insult to every self-respecting Jew right into the nineteenth century.

How is Mendelssohn's apparently feeble attitude in this matter to be explained? Was it fear of the Jews or fear of the government? It could not be the former for the total abolition of the oath in its offensive form would have pleased every section of the Jewish community, while by recommending a German version of the admonition he knew he would arouse the wrath and hatred of the rabbinical Jews. Some of the rabbis, like the rabbi of Fürth, reacted by publicly and officially cursing Mendelssohn for advocating the German version. From the government he had nothing to fear. He enjoyed the greatest respect in government circles and the same Frederick who in 1778 abolished the vexatious inspectorship of the Königsberg synagogue might have consented to abolish the odious and at the same time futile oath if strong representations had been made to that effect by Mendelssohn.

The explanation is probably that Mendelssohn was at heart a pacifist and, with regard to the destiny of his people, a fatalist. His was, however, a fatalism based on an unbounded faith in the promises of Jehovah. If it was God's purpose that the Jews should suffer centuries of humiliation and persecution such tribulations had to be borne patiently as long as life and limb were safe and the Jews were free to worship in their own manner. Whenever he interceded for his people these were the considerations which guided him. Beyond these limits he was not even interested. When his friend Abt asked him in 1764 what was to become of the Jews he replied: "You ask me concerning the destination of my countrymen? What countrymen? those of Dessau or those of Jerusalem? Make yourself clearer and I shall say with Molière's Pancratius: 'Je m'en lave les mains. Je n'en sais rien. Il en sera ce qu'il en pourra. Selon les aventures.' Whatever does not interfere with my system does not worry me. Pompadour, Brühl, the Jesuits, inquisitors, pirates, tyrants, poisoners and traitors; what does all that matter? With the composure of a German metaphysician I wrap myself in my threadbare cloak and I say like Pangloss: 'This world is the best of all.' "

XXI

A TRANSLATION AND ITS CONSEQUENCES

We must not forget that the letter quoted at the end of the preceding chapter was written in 1764 and does not altogether represent Mendelssohn's attitude towards the Jewish question in his later years when his almost cynically cheerful *laisser aller* policy gives way to a very deep concern about the low cultural condition of his people. This modifies his fatalism to some extent. He had himself benefited by his close contact with German culture without ceasing to be a good Jew. He felt that the jargon his people spoke and which few Germans could understand, along with the Jewish horro: of profane knowledge were the main causes of the lamentable condition of the Jews. He could find no scriptural warrant for ignorance and as the Jewish-German dialect was not Hebrew he could see nothing sacred in it. The surrounding German culture was far above that of the Jews and the chasm dividing them was widening at an alarming rate. The only hope for the Jews lay in discarding Judeo-German and adopting pure German instead.

Mendelssohn had always spoken German with his wife and children and the latter had to learn Hebrew as a foreign language if they were to read the Scriptures in the original. To facilitate the study of the Hebrew Scriptures for his children, Mendelssohn began his German translation of the Pentateuch. The plan of his life, he tells Hennings in 1779, had originally been to manufacture silk materials during the day and woo the caresses of philosophy in his leisure hours. It had pleased Providence to lead him along a different path. "As the result of Lavater's obtrusion," he adds, "I had lost the capacity to meditate and with it the greater part of my contentment. After some reflection I found however that the remainder of my strength might suffice to render a service to my children and perhaps to a considerable portion of my people by furnishing them with a better translation and commentary of the sacred books than they had had hitherto. This is a first step towards a culture from which my people has been kept away to such an extent that we might almost despair of the possibility of improvement. Still I considered myself obliged to do what little I could and to leave the rest to Providence which often takes more time to carry out its plans than we can calculate."

Translation and commentary were taken in hand in 1778 and the whole was finished five years later. If Mendelssohn in his more ambitious moments had ever dreamed of translating the whole of the Old Testament, the five years spent on the Pentateuch alone must have shown him the hopelessness of his dream. He had a number of scholars like Dubno, Wessely and Homburg to help him especially in writing the Hebrew commentary, but the main burden of the task naturally lay on his shoulders and his strength was limited. Besides, the undertaking was not free from financial difficulties as Mendelssohn, not desiring to derive any pecuniary profit, had fixed a very low price for his translation.

The success exceeded all expectations and orders came in from all parts of Europe. Among the subscribers were several crowned heads such as the King and the Crown Prince of Denmark. The latter, however, seems to have been tormented by serious doubts regarding the respectability of a translation of the Scriptures made by a Jew living in the rationalistic Berlin. So the Danish minister, Hoegh Guldberg, ordered his master's copy only on the understanding that "the work contained nothing contrary to the majesty and truth of Holy Scripture as His Royal Highness would be shocked if he found he had subscribed to a scandalous work!"

As the translation was printed in Hebrew characters the Christians naturally showed little interest. Even when for their benefit the book of Genesis was printed in German type the demand was so discouraging that the work of transliteration was discontinued. One Christian reviewer [1] calls the publication a memorable event, "possibly so far the noblest version of the Pentateuch." He would like to see the translation of the whole of the Old Testament done in the same way which would be a joy for the Christians and a blessing for the Jews. He adds however: "We doubt whether among the author's coreligionists in Germany there are many who understand his German. I have placed what has appeared so far before some by no means ignorant Jews but they experienced some difficulty in reading the German and understanding it."

Mendelssohn's Pentateuch received a very mixed reception at the hands of his coreligionists. Even those among them "who had difficulty in reading the German and understanding it" grasped the deep significance of the innovation, but they expected terrible or beneficial consequences according to the standpoint they took up and they damned or extolled the translator accordingly. The whole of the Berlin rabbinate evinced the most flattering appreciation and the Chief Rabbi, Hirschel Levin, granted the *imprimatur* with the utmost readiness. They all realized what a disgrace it was for Judaism that its schoolmasters knew neither Hebrew nor German and they expected great things from that German translation and its Hebrew commentary. Other rabbis

---

[1] In Doederlein's *Theologische Bibliothek,* quoted by Kayserling.

especially those with pronounced Polish affiliations were just as emphatic in their opposition. This was natural enough. A Polish rabbi would see that his craft was in danger. If the use of German spread among the Jews the rabbis would have to go back to school and learn German or do something else for their living. No doubt there were to be found also among the opposition some honest unselfish souls to whom Hebrew though unintelligible to the great majority of the Jews was yet a sacred language and as such, whether intelligible or not, necessary unto salvation. They saw in the introduction of German outside the synagogue the thin end of the wedge for the supplanting of Hebrew by German in the religious services. They were perfectly right. Soon the demand for the use of German within the synagogue became so insistent, by the beginning of the nineteenth century the preaching, singing and praying in German had increased so alarmingly that the orthodox Jews were reduced to intriguing against their own coreligionists. In answer to their complaint Frederick William III issued an order forbidding the use of any language except Hebrew in the Jewish service. Seeing that by that time the number of Jews understanding Hebrew had been reduced to a mere handful, the order cannot have added much to the attractiveness of the Jewish service.

Of the peril to the unity of Judaism lurking in

his German version of the Pentateuch, Mendelssohn
had not, of course, the faintest suspicion. Nor did
any doubt enter his mind regarding the cheerful
optimism of those who imagined that a Hebrew
commentary appended to the German translation
would make the Jews undergo the additional labour
of learning a difficult language like Hebrew which
was useless outside the synagogue. At the back of
the rabbinical opposition Mendelssohn saw nothing
but ignorance, blindness and obstinacy. Its very
existence proved that he was right. "If my translation," he wrote in 1781, "had been accepted by all
Jews without a protest I should have thought it
superfluous. The more the so-called wise men of our
time oppose it, the more necessary it is. I wrote it
at first for the common man, but now I find that
the rabbis need it even more, and I am ready, if God
is willing and grants me his help, to translate the
prophets and hagiographers as well."

Mendelssohn was not mistaken with regard to the
cultural importance and effect of his work. His Pentateuch was undoubtedly for many the bridge across
the chasm and led them to a higher culture. It might
even be said to have bridged two chasms, for Mendelssohn's translations restored to the Jews at least
a portion of their ancient inheritance from which
they had so long been shut out by an unintelligible
language and latterly by an absurd conception of the
aim and function of education. Under the régime of

the Polish Talmudists the Scriptures had become almost as unknown as the language in which they were written. Jewish ignorance in this respect was stupendous. Their Polish teachers, "the most ignorant of all idiots," as Kayserling calls them, gave them nothing beyond ridiculously subtle, fanciful, hair-splitting interpretations and left them in total darkness regarding the thing interpreted.

Once the contact with the surrounding German culture was established, further developments followed logically. German replacing Yiddish sealed the Polish teacher's doom. Throughout Germany there had always been individual cases of Jews being admitted to German schools and universities. Now, more than ever, progressive Jews cast longing glances towards institutions in which not only German was taught but where the curriculum was laid out along more generous lines than in Jewish schools where most things really worth knowing were taboo. The slow rate of speed with which such yearning was crystallized into action disappointed the more impatient optimists who forgot that they were dealing with human material impeded by century-old traditions and habits and that cultural movements are not carried out after the manner of an earthquake. Mainly through the munificence of the Prince of Dessau an educational institution had been founded in 1774 at Dessau by Basedow, the educational reformer. It was called the *Philanthropin* and

the pedagogic system was based on the educational
principles of Rousseau. In the admission of pupils
there was to be no discrimination on the score of
religion. In spite of the invitation to Jewish parents
to send their boys there and the promise that very
distinguished Jewish boys could aspire to become
teachers in the school, the Jewish pupils failed to
present themselves and the financial support coming
from Jews was disappointing. In time, of course,
this state of things was remedied. Jewish pupils arrived and even the subscriptions came in, though
without undue haste.

Mendelssohn, who knew the situation and the mentality of his coreligionists better than anybody, declined to become the echo of the complaints about
Jewish apathy coming, among others, from the
Christian founders and directors of the school. He
showed his wisdom by advising the complainants
not only to be patient but even to be very careful
in admitting Jewish applicants and to take only the
most promising. He knew that in spite of the atmosphere of absolute equality it was planned to
create, only the brightest Jewish boys could hope to
combat by their achievements the inveterate conviction of the racial inferiority of the Jews among
their fellow-pupils.

One of the most interesting results of Mendelssohn's educational ideas was the establishment in
1781 of the first German school for Jews in Ger-

many, the *Jüdische Freischule*. The teachers were Jews and Christians and the curriculum comprised the study of Bible and Talmud, French, German, bookkeeping, physical geography. Schools after this model were in the course of time set up in Breslau, Dessau, Frankfurt, Seesen and other places. The Jews were thus fitting themselves to enter the German commonwealth on a basis of cultural equality. What were they going to do with their education when once they had acquired it? Would they continue to be pedlars and dealers in old clothes? Obviously it was for the Christians to make the next move.

XXII

A PLEA FOR THE JEWS

In spite of his aversion to religious polemics, Mendelssohn again became the storm centre of a controversy the very year in which he finished his labours on the Pentateuch, in 1783. It was his last great battle in defence of his religion.

The Alsatian Jews who were subjects of France had petitioned Mendelssohn through their spokesman Cerf Beer, to draw up a memorial setting forth the intolerable oppression under which they were suffering. Mendelssohn was at the time very busy on his translation, so he asked his friend Wilhelm Dohm, a young man who had already got a name as a promising writer on political topics, to take the matter in hand. This he consented to do, but not being specially interested in the Alsatian Jews he took up the wider question of Jewish disabilities and produced a very remarkable work which he called *On the Civil Emancipation of the Jews*. He combats the general impression that the Jewish character unfits the Jew for citizenship in European states. He maintains that all the Jew is reproached with can be explained as the natural and necessary

MOSES MENDELSSOHN
(*Painted by Frisch. Lithograph by L. Sachse*)

consequence of his hostile environment, the oppression and persecution which fall to his lot in European countries. His energy on the other hand, his sagacity, industry, adaptability, the loyalty he has ever shown to his ancient religion which showed the strength of his character would be so many assets in a modern state. Dohm then demands a series of reforms tending to the complete emancipation of the Jews: religious equality with all other subjects, admission to industrial pursuits, special encouragement for Jews to engage in handicrafts and agriculture, abolition of every restriction tending to bar them from artistic or scientific occupations, reform of their education, improvement of their schools, admission to certain offices of the state and in the civic administration, and at the same time the granting of a certain measure of autonomy in civil matters relating to the religious statutes. In connection with the demand for religious liberty he claims for every religious community the right to suspend dissentient members or even expel them but without prejudice to their civil status.[1]

As Dohm was about a hundred years ahead of his time, it may be imagined that some of his contemporaries stood aghast and the author and his

[1] The brightest and toughest of French red tape was responsible for the six hundred copies of Dohm's work, which had been translated into French, never reaching the Conseil d'Etat. As the package arrived at the frontier and as it was not accompanied by a permit, it was, though addressed to the Conseil d'Etat, confiscated, sent to the Bastille and finally destroyed.

work were made the objective of numerous attacks. That any man in his senses could make such proposals appeared to them so incomprehensible, almost so revolting, that there could only be one explanation: the author had been handsomely bribed by the Jews. Others trotted out all the accusations that had ever been made against the Jews and had so often been controverted effectively. Professor Michaelis of Göttingen who had already achieved distinction on another occasion by stating that "a noble Jew was a poetic impossibility" [2] again threw himself into the fray. It was a hopeful sign of the times that Dohm's proposals, or most of them, met with a good deal of approval among the thinking portion of the community. Mendelssohn felt great joy at the thought that "an all-kind Providence had let him live long enough to see the day when people were beginning to take the rights of humanity to heart." Nevertheless the controversy had shown that even among cultured people there were still to be found the haziest notions regarding the Jews, their character and their religion, that Mendelssohn felt that he could not remain an onlooker, but must take part in the fight.

He got his friend Marcus Herz to translate Menasse Ben Israel's *Plea for the Jews* [3] from Eng-

---

[2] In his review of Lessing's *Der Jude.*

[3] *The Plea for the Jews* (Vindiciæ Iudæorum) was written in 1655 by Menasse Ben Israel to defend the English Jews against the attacks made by the Anglican and Catholic clergy.

lish into German under the title *Rettung der Juden.*
To this translation he wrote his *Preface.* It is interesting to see the same Mendelssohn who had
once been so sure that "any scholar was welcome
to the most ludicrous conception of Judaism without the slightest contradiction from him" expressing himself with very excusable bitterness on the
subject of precisely that ludicrous conception of
Judaism of which he once spoke with such equanim-
ity. As he grew older he became ever more conscious of his solidarity with the rest of the Jews.
Situated as he was with an assured income, an honoured place in the world of letters and a comparative
immunity from the evil effects of both Christian
and Jewish bigotry he had on the whole little to
complain of. Anti-Jewish legislation hardly touched
him now personally. But he saw around him thousands of coreligionists whose lives were made wellnigh unbearable by oppressive restrictions which met
them at every turn. He had remained an orthodox
Jew and his ethical decency forbade him to enjoy
a peace and comfort from which others were barred
for no better reason than that they held precisely
the same convictions that were sacred to him. "It
is curious to see," he said in one of the opening
paragraphs of his *Preface,* "what different forms
prejudice assumes throughout the centuries to op-
press us and to place difficulties in the way of our
reception as citizens. In superstitious days we were

charged with frivolous desecration, piercing cruci-fixes to make them bleed, secretly circumcising Christian children, shedding Christian blood for our Passover ceremonies, poisoning of wells and so on. We were accused of unbelief, obstinacy, practising secret arts and devilries, on account of which we were tortured, deprived of our possessions, driven into exile, if not executed. . . . Nowadays we are re-proached with superstition and stupidity, want of moral feeling, taste, refined manners, inaptitude for the arts, sciences, useful industries, for service in the army and the state, invincible disposition to fraud, usury and lawlessness, which have taken the place of the cruder accusations to exclude us from among the number of useful citizens. Formerly peo-ple took infinite trouble to turn us, not into useful citizens, but into Christians, but as we obstinately refused to be converted this was considered a suf-ficient reason for looking upon us as a useless burden and for attributing to the abandoned monsters all the abominations that would expose us to the hatred and contempt of all men. Now this ardour to con-vert us has cooled. We are completely neglected. Christians continue to keep us away from arts, sci-ences and useful industries, all the roads to useful improvement are blocked and our lack of culture is made a ground for further oppression. They tie our hands and then blame us for not using them."

He by no means falls in with all the reforms proposed by Dohm. He vehemently protests against the suggestion that religious communities should have the right to suspend and even expel dissentient members without prejudice to their civil status. The words "ecclesiastical rights," "ecclesiastical power" convey no clear meaning to his mind. There is no such thing as power over opinions and convictions. "True, divine religion," he says, "knows no other power but the power to win and convince with the help of reasons and to render happy by convincing. It needs neither arms nor fingers for its use, it is all spirit and heart." How can any body of men dictate opinions relating to eternal truth? How can any church exclude those who desire to take part in its devotional exercises without running counter to its own aim and object? He finds that the wisest among his ancestors have laid no claim to the right of exclusion from religious services and he quotes in support a passage from Solomon's prayer spoken on the occasion of the dedication of the temple: "Concerning a stranger that is not of thy people, Israel, but cometh out of a far country for thy name's sake, when he shall come and pray towards this house hear thou in heaven, thy dwelling place, and do according to all that the stranger calleth to thee for."

As for Dohm's demand that exclusion from a religious community should be without prejudice to the civil status of the person penalized Mendelssohn

shows this to be chimerical. He looks upon this stipu-
lation as hopelessly ineffective to act as a safeguard.
It is granted generally that an expelled member of
a religious community may all the same be a useful
and respected citizen and deeply religious. To de-
prive such a man of all opportunity to manifest
his religion outwardly by taking part in the devotional exercises of a divine service of his religion is
an unbearable idea. "How can the state decree," he
asks, "that a useful and respected citizen should be
made unhappy by law?" Further he inquires: "What
would ecclesiastical exclusion be without civic consequences, without influence on the respect he enjoys outside the church, on the good reputation of
the expelled person, on the confidence of his fellow
citizens without which no one can carry on his calling and be useful to the state? . . . Introducing
church discipline and at the same time safeguarding
civil happiness seems to me to be a problem which
still awaits solution in politics. It is like breaking the
cask without spilling the wine!"

Mendelssohn spoke particularly feelingly on this
topic as the rabbis of his time, so far from emulat-
ing Solomon's generous attitude, were as bigoted as
anything to be found in Europe. The case of Samuel
Marcus of Hamburg who was excommunicated
probably for some form of dissent and the ridiculous
and despotic penalties imposed upon him was still
fresh in everybody's memory. Mendelssohn enter-

tained a wholesome distrust of every kind of clergy. "No clergy," he says, "is as yet sufficiently enlightened to be safely entrusted with such a right."

An astonishing number of liberal Christian theologians like Spalding, Teller and Zollikofer expressed their perfect agreement with the author of the *Preface* though they were fairly balanced by dissentient voices. The most judicious critic was the anonymous author of *The Search for Light and Right,* who declared himself in complete accord with Mendelssohn on the question of ecclesiastical power. He maintained, however, that Mendelssohn's view was entirely contrary to what he understood to be the very foundation of Judaism, that by contraverting the ecclesiastical law given by Moses which claimed to be founded on divine revelation he endangered the whole edifice of the Jewish religion. "Was this," he asked, "Mendelssohn's first step towards the fulfilment of the wish expressed by Lavater?" Mendelssohn felt that a much fuller statement of his case was required to set at rest such doubts. So he wrote his *Jerusalem or Ecclesiastical Authority and Judaism* (Jerusalem, oder über religiöse nacht und Judenthum).

XXIII

MENDELSSOHN ON CHURCH
AND STATE

The first part deals with the function and rights of the state, a favourite theme of discussion at the time. Locke's definition of the state as a society of men, who unite for the purpose of promoting their temporal welfare and therefore not concerned with the religion of its members is rather too sweeping for Mendelssohn who was always disinclined to carry his logical conclusions to the bitter end. State and Church are at one with regard to their aim, the promotion of human happiness, he says. But the state is concerned with the relations of men and God. The means also of carrying out their respective intentions are different. The state being charged with the duty of ensuring order and security is equipped with the power to compel and to override individual opinion in the interest of the whole. Religion, on the other hand, does not recognize acts unaccompanied by conviction. Religious acts without religious thoughts are vain trifling, not divine service. These religious acts must originate in the spirit and can neither be bought with rewards nor enforced by punishments. Religion knows no compulsion. The state orders and compels, religion instructs and persuades; the state gives laws, religion commandments. The state has at its disposal physical force, the power of religion is love and charity. The state may give up the disobedient and expel him, the church takes him to its heart and seeks to instruct or at least comfort him to the very last moment of his life.

The state must not mix itself up with religious controversies nor favour any particular set of doctrines. The right of interference with religions or religious sects Mendelssohn grants to the state only in regard to those principles which threaten the ethical or social foundations of the state itself. It is again very characteristic of Mendelssohn who without any apparent logical necessity will always go so far and no further. He would allow the state to proceed against Atheism, Epicurism and Fanaticism. Atheism constitutes a danger to the state because "without belief in God, Providence and a future life happiness is a mere dream, virtue ceases to be virtue, the love of humanity becomes a mere weakness, benevolence is little more than foppery." Mendelssohn does not see that this is, of course, contrary to both reason and experience. The same blindness is found in much of the Enlightenment Philosophy of the eighteenth century. It is an attitude born partly of intellectual and social timidity and partly of the fundamental axiom that the object of all philosophy is the happiness of mankind, that the universe was created for the happiness of mankind and that the test of truth is happiness. Anything increasing our unhappiness must therefore be false. The ultimate test of truth is thus the philosopher's feeling of what would contribute to his own happiness and what would not. Mendelssohn imagines that as an atheist he would be profoundly unhappy. That settles the question.

The result of all the above differentiation between the object and method of state action and ecclesiastical action is that the only rational modus vivendi between church and state is a friendly parallelism. Convergence of their lines of action is fraught with danger. There must be no interdependence. The state must never become the tool of the church to carry out its behests. Any church that cannot perform its functions by means of instruction and persuasion only and relies on the strong arm of the state is a failure. As in the *Preface,* he protests against the right of exclusion and excommunication claimed by religious bodies with the additional plea that among those who have in the past been excommunicated you will find more true religion than among the crowd who expelled them. In the end we find Mendelssohn denying ministers of religion all claim to material rewards, benefits or power, granting them only compensation for loss of time. Clearly, according to him, the state is to have power, the church only influence.

In the second part he answers the contention of critics of his *Preface* who maintained that by such separation of church and state he was undermining the very foundations of Judaism as in the Jewish theocracy religion had ever leant on the strong arm of the law.

Mendelssohn distinguishes three things in Judaism. These are first, doctrines of eternal truths regarding God and his reign and Providence without which men can be neither enlightened nor happy. God makes known these truths, he says, to all men at all times and in all places clearly and unmistakably through their reason. They are thus not revealed in the ordinary sense of the word. Secondly, there are historical truths giving information about the past of the Jewish people and dependent for their credibility on the authority of the different writers which, of course, is merely a matter of historical inquiry. So far, then, we have not a distinct religion, certainly not a revealed religion, for the religious or metaphysical element in Judaism is nothing more than natural religion common to all men and founded on reason. What distinguishes Judaism from any other natural religion is that it has in addition a set of laws, precepts, commandments and rules of living peculiar to itself, relating to conduct, not to belief, and binding on the Jews only. These laws were given by God not as the creator and preserver of the universe but as the protector and ally of the ancestors of the Jews, as the deliverer, founder, captain, king and chief of this people. They are necessary for the salvation of the Jews, the rest of humanity can attain salvation without them. All that is necessary in the case of the latter is virtuous conduct founded on the eternal and universally acceptable truths of natural religion demonstrated by reason and neither revealed nor authenticated by miracles. Among all the Jewish laws there is not one saying: "Thou shalt believe" or "Thou shalt not believe;" all say: "Thou shalt do or not do." No orders are given to faith which accepts only orders which reach it by the way of conviction. All the commandments of the divine law are addressed to the will, to the energy of man. Indeed in Hebrew the word which is generally translated by "faith" means in most places no more than "trust" or "confidence." There is no passage saying: "Believe, Israel, thou wilt be blest; do not doubt Israel, or this or that punishment will be inflicted on thee!" Command and prohibition, reward and punishment are for acts, of commission or omission, which depend on a man's will and are governed by notions of good or evil, by hope and fear. Belief or doubt, assent or dissent are not governed by our desires, by fear or hope, but by our perception of truth or falsehood. Ancient Judaism has, therefore, no articles of faith, no symbolical books. "The spirit of Judaism," he says in a letter written in 1782, "is conformity in acts but liberty with regard to doctrines." So that, according to Mendelssohn, the Jew has perfect freedom of belief, but is bound to yield the strictest obedience to the ceremonial law, the only revealed part of his religion.

The unsophisticated non-Jew may perhaps be excused for looking upon this distinction as somewhat of a quibble. The assertion that the Deity commanded the Jews to carry out the 613 practices prescribed by the ceremonial law is, strictly considered, just as much a dogma as the dogma of the virgin birth of Jesus. The plea that the former makes a stronger appeal to our reason, while readily admitted, does not establish a fundamental difference. If all the 613 were founded on reason it would, but in that case, the need for revelation would disappear. Now Mendelssohn admits that the rational grounds cannot in all cases be perceived, hence the need of faith in these rules as revealed by a higher being. Thus they become so many dogmas as to their origin and, as the result, Mendelssohn's perfect freedom of belief vanishes. It is true the Mosaic law does not impose a penalty on the denial of the existence of the Deity, but it makes death by stoning the punishment for sabbath-breaking, i. e. for disobedience to a precept of the ceremonial law. We imagine that it made little difference to the person about to be stoned whether he was executed for the sake of a doctrine that was explicitly a dogma or one only implicitly so.

Mendelssohn's argument does not become more convincing when he pleads as follows: "Originally state and religion were not united, they were one; they were not joined together, they were one and the same thing. The relation of man to society and the relation of man to God converged and could never find themselves in conflict. God, the creator and preserver of the world, was at the same time the king and governor of this nation. . . . Civil matters with the Jews assumed a sacred and religious aspect and every service rendered to the state was a divine service. The community was the community of God, its affairs were those of God and everything down to the simplest police regulation partook of the nature of divine service. Thus every offence against the authority of God as the legislator of the nation was lèse-majesté and therefore a crime against the state. . . . Whoever desecrated the sabbath abrogated as far as in him lay, a fundamental law of civil society, for an essential part of the constitution was based on the institution of the sabbath which God had given expressly as an eternal covenant between himself and the Children of srael. Under such a constitution these crimes h: to be punished by the civil authorities, not as er neous opinions, not as unbelief, but as misdeeds, as criminal offences which tended to abrogate or to weaken the authority of the lawgiver and thereby to undermine the state itself."

This was the state of things in the Jewish homeland. Since the destruction of the Temple all capital punishment, imprisonment and even money fines have ceased to be lawful. The ties that bound the nation together have been severed, offences against religion are no longer offences against the state and religion as such knows of no punishment, of no penance other than the one the penitent sinner voluntarily imposes upon himself.

The result of Mendelssohn's argument appears to be that in Palestinian times religion as such had neither the right nor the power to inflict temporal punishment on unbelief or erroneous opinion. Indeed it could not have separate rights and powers of any kind as religion and state were one and the same thing. Since the Jewish state ceased to exist, there remains now only the Jewish religion and when Mendelssohn insists on the separation of church and state as a general principle for safeguarding religious liberty in modern times he cannot be charged with undermining Judaism or shaking the foundations of a Jewish theocracy which no longer exists. Whatever we may think of individual portions of his argument, of his claim that the Jews enjoy perfect freedom of belief with regard to everything excepting the validity of the law, of the restriction he imposes on the freedom of belief of others with regard to the existence of God, etc., he has undoubtedly shown that it is quite possible to be an orthodox Jew and yet both enjoy and grant to others a generous measure of religious and philosophical freedom of thought. It was perhaps fortunate for the validity of his argument that it never occurred to him to discuss the interesting question why, if Jewish religion and Jewish state were one and indivisible, the religion did not fall along with the state.

At the end he admonishes the Jews to resign themselves to the manners and constitution of the land in which they have been placed but at the same time to hold fast to the religion of their fathers and bear the burdens of both, no matter how irksome the difference of climate and time may render the observance of their law. He cannot see how anyone born of the house of Jacob can conscientiously put aside the law until the all highest law-giver abrogates it as clearly and as publicly as he gave it. Even if a Jew went over to the Christian religion he would have to carry the law with him. Of the Christians he asks civil recognition. But if equality can be obtained only at the price of the surrender of Jewish allegiance to their ancient law he will have none of it. The Jews will in that case ask only for alleviation of their burdens and to be considered and treated if not as fellow-citizens at least as fellow-men and fellow-inhabitants. With a union of the

two faiths, a compromise such as had been proposed
by some, he will have nothing to do. The idea of one
flock and one shepherd does not mean that the whole
flock is to graze in the same field. A union of faiths
would not mean toleration, it would mean the very
opposite.

It was one of the most significant signs of the
time that a member of the most despised and oppressed people on earth should raise his voice to
claim the rights of common humanity. There was
nothing very revolutionary about his manner of asking, but it was none the less impressive. Never had
intolerance and state interference in religious matters been so lucidly shown to be utterly devoid of all
rational basis. Kant called *Jerusalem* an irrefutable
book. "I consider this book," he wrote to Mendelssohn, "to be the announcement of a great reform
moving forward no matter how slowly, a reform
which will affect not only your nation but also
others. You have known how to combine with your
religion a degree of liberty of conscience we should
never have thought possible and which no other religion can boast of. You have so clearly and thoroughly demonstrated the necessity of unrestricted
liberty of conscience in every religion that our church
will have to think of freeing its religion of all that burdens and oppresses conscience, which must ultimately
unite all men in the essentials of religion. All religious
tenets burden conscience if acceptance of their truth

is made the condition of salvation." All Christian theologians were deeply interested and the book became the theme of heated controversy. That Herder, who was himself a high official in the state church, should show little enthusiasm for that part of *Jerusalem* which deals with the separation of church and state is very natural, and it was also to be expected that Professor Michaelis of Göttingen should beat his antisemitic tomtom with accustomed energy. Altogether the references to *Jerusalem* showed a surprising variety of standpoint, some calling Mendelssohn a rabbinical orthodox Jew and others an atheist.

The Jews, on the whole, derived much comfort from *Jerusalem*. The orthodox were pleased with the author's uncompromising insistence on the continued validity of the ceremonial law, while the more sceptical were equally delighted with what they interpreted as an assurance that provided they observed the law they need not believe anything. It is at least doubtful whether the Jews at the time grasped the full significance of *Jerusalem*. On the other hand it is perfectly certain that the author did not see all its logical consequences.

XXIV

THE MORNING HOURS

Mendelssohn's last work of any importance was his *Morning Hours* (Morgenstunden). Just as he had written his translation of the Pentateuch in the first place for the benefit of his children so *Morning Hours* is the record of notes he used in instructing his eldest son Joseph in the "rational knowledge of God." Other young people, his daughter Dorothea and her husband Simon Veit and the two brothers Humboldt, were also privileged to profit by these talks and discussions which were given early in the morning, this being the only time of the day when he felt sufficiently well for his task. When he published these talks he prefixed to them a preface which begins with the following pathetic admission: "These discourses on the existence of God contain the result of all I have in the past read and thought about this important subject of inquiry. For the last twelve or fifteen years I have found myself utterly unable to enlarge my philosophical knowledge. A form of neurasthenia to which I am subject forbade all mental effort. The works of the great men who have since appeared in metaphysics, Lambert, Tetens,

Platner and the titanic Kant I know only from the inadequate reports of my friends or from the learned reviews which are rarely much more instructive. As far as I am concerned this science stands where it stood about the seventy-fifth year of the present century. However much it cost me I have never been able to bid philosophy farewell for good though I have been obliged to keep away from her for many years. Alas! in better days philosophy was my most faithful companion, my only consolation in all the adversities of life. Now I must avoid her everywhere like a deadly enemy, or what is still harder, shun her like a pest-ridden friend who warns me to avoid her society. I have not always had the self-abnegation to obey her. There have been from time to time clandestine transgressions, although never without repentance and expiation."

Seven of the seventeen chapters are devoted to an examination of truth, appearance and error. They seek to supply an answer to the question: what is truth? The remaining chapters deal with the main task he has set himself, namely proving the existence of God, the necessary and absolutely perfect Being. Of all the different proofs that have been attempted in the past by philosophers and theologians the ontological seems to him to hold out the greatest prospect of success. It is certainly the one offering the most brilliant opportunities to his really remarkable dialectical skill. Briefly, this method of proof concludes the reality of a thing from the clearness and logical consistency of the idea we have of it. "Whatever is not," he says, "must be either impossible or merely possible. If it is impossible it is so because it involves a contradiction. If it is only possible its reality depends on some other reality, i. e. it is dependent. This is incompatible with our conception of the most perfect Being, for an independent existence is more perfect than a dependent one. The most perfect Being is therefore either real or involves a contradiction. And as the idea of a most perfect Being does not involve a contradiction, therefore the most perfect Being exists. As someone has pointed out: this is the same method of arguing as if we said: 'This is the most beautiful story I ever read, therefore it must be true. If it is not true then the truest story, no matter how insignificant, must appear to me to be the most beautiful.'"

There is no very triumphant note in the paragraphs which follow this argument. We can almost sense a suspicion lurking in his mind regarding the adequacy and cogency of his argumentation. The subsequent elaboration of the proof is meant to counter the objection of those who refuse to conclude reality from the mere idea and it culminates in the Leibnitzian: "All that is has truth and highest excellence; all that has truth and highest excellence must really be."

On the whole, the book makes dull reading. There

is no longer the joyous freshness and the lightness of touch of his earlier philosophical writings. His method of proof is often laboured and far from convincing. He was, however, still able to impress his hearers deeply by the warmth of his conviction which, combined with the lovable character of the man, would probably not allow his youthful pupils to see the awkward gaps in his argumentation.

In the *Morning Hours* Mendelssohn was fighting a losing battle and he realized it with some bitterness. Five years before that, in 1781, Kant had examined the proofs hitherto given for the existence of a Deity and shown their hopeless logical inadequacy. To those who had read Kant, Mendelssohn's demonstration must have seemed like a voice from the dead.

XXV

THE WEARY SWORDSMAN

The last years of Mendelssohn's life were the unhappiest in many respects. His friend Lessing died in 1781 and Mendelssohn, though he still had a large circle of friends, had among them none to take the place left vacant by Lessing's death. For a number of years past even his relations with Lessing had been rendered less perfect by several jarring notes. They had no longer seen eye to eye in philosophic and religious questions. Lessing's publication of the Reimarus Fragments had deeply wounded Mendelssohn by their bitter attack on the historical foundations of his religion and their crudely irreverent criticism of the patriarchs and heroes of the Jewish people, and in the course of their argument concerning the secrets of Freemasonry Mendelssohn had shown an irritability out of proportion to the importance of the point at issue. In the whole of the life and death struggle between Lessing and bigoted orthodoxy as represented by Pastor Goetze which arose out of the publication of the Fragments, Mendelssohn stood unsympathetically aside and looked upon Lessing's gigantic polemics as mere wran-

gling (Zänkereien). Lessing's great soul resigned itself to such occasional dissonance as the inevitable
concomitant of all search for truth. What hurt him
was not that his friend differed from him but that he
would not agree to differ. In the last letter he wrote
to Mendelssohn he shows how clearly he realizes that
they have drifted far apart. In the battle he had waged
for freedom of thought he had been subjected to
worse persecution than had ever fallen to the lot of his
Jewish friend. He was profoundly discouraged and
he had come to see that all positive religion was mischievous. The letter was written a few months before his death to introduce a Jew, Alexander Davison,
who had been persecuted by both Jews and Christians.
"All he wants from you," he says, "is that you should
show him the shortest and safest road to some European country where there are neither Christians nor
Jews. I hate to lose him, but as soon as he has safely
arrived there I shall be the first to follow him. . . . I
am still chewing and enjoying the letter you sent me
through Dr. Flies. Indeed, dear friend, I need such
a letter from time to time if I am not to become
altogether morose. You know that I am not a man
who is hungering for praise. But the coldness with
which the world is wont to treat certain persons
who do not seem to be able to do anything right,
is, if not fatal, at least paralysing. That you are not
pleased with everything I have written for some
time past does not surprise me in the least. None of

it could have pleased you, for it was not written for you. At most a page here and there could have misled you by a memory of our better days. I too was then a healthy young tree and now I am a gnarled and rotten trunk. Ah, dear friend, the play is finished. Yet I should like to talk to you once more."

It was the last letter of a correspondence at one time so animated and stimulating, but which had become distressfully intermittent, showing longer and ever longer intervals and often threatening to lapse altogether. Before Mendelssohn could reply to this last sign of life or carry out his friend's wish that they should meet once more he received the news that Lessing was dead. He was overwhelmed with a grief which found expression a few days later in a letter to Lessing's brother Karl. All the differences which had threatened their friendship are forgotten, the memory of all the irritation his friend's uncompromising radicalism had caused him has faded away; he only remembers the great teacher to whom he owed so much and whom future ages only will understand. "Not a word, my friend," he begins his letter, "of our loss, of the great defeat our hearts have suffered. The memory of the man we have lost is too sacred to be desecrated by lamentations. He appears to me now in a light which diffuses repose and cheerfulness over all around it. No, I no longer consider what I lost through his departure. I render heartfelt thanks to Providence for the blessing, that in the strength of my youth I have been privileged to know a man who has formed my mind, whom in every act I planned, every line I wrote, I could look upon as a friend and a judge and whom at all times in future I shall take for my friend and judge whenever I propose to take a step of any importance. If any sadness mingles with this thought, it is perhaps due to remorse that I have not always taken full advantage of his guidance, that I did not crave more greedily for his instructive intercourse, that I neglected many an hour in which I might have benefited by his conversation. Alas! his conversation was an abundant spring from which one could unceasingly draw ideas of the Good and the Beautiful which gushed forth like common water for the use of all. The liberality with which he gave his opinion sometimes exposed me to the risk of misjudging his merit, for it seemed to cost him no effort. Sometimes he so managed to substitute his views for mine that I could no longer distinguish them. Altogether his generosity was not of the narrow-minded kind of the rich who make you feel that they are giving alms. Rather he stimulated your industry and let you earn what he gave you.

"All things considered, my friend, your brother has departed at the right moment, not only at the right moment according to the plan of the universe, for according to that everything happens at the right moment but also within our narrow sphere. Fontenelle said of Copernicus: he made known his system and died. The biographer will be able to say of your brother: he wrote *Nathan the Wise* and died. I can form no conception of any work which would excel *Nathan* as in my eyes this work excels everything Lessing had written until then. He could not rise higher without reaching a region where he would pass beyond our bodily vision. This he has done. Now we stand like the disciples of the prophet and contemplate the spot from which he rose on high and vanished. A few weeks before his decease I had occasion to warn him not to be surprised if the great mass of his contemporaries misjudged the merits of this work. A better posterity would fifty years after his death still find much to chew and digest in his *Nathan*. He was indeed more than a century ahead of his time."

Unfortunately Mendelssohn was not left to the peaceful enjoyment of the memories of his friend as anticipated in the letter just quoted. To defend Lessing from what he considered to be vile and unjust aspersions he let himself be involved in a last and bitter controversy the issue of which was from the very first rendered at least doubtful by the fact that the champion of Lessing was neither physically nor mentally quite equal to his task. The condition of his health at the time made rest, absence of all mental effort and freedom from worry and excitement imperative and the discussion of the point at issue in the controversy, the relation of Lessing to the philosophy of Spinoza, presupposed a sympathetic understanding of Pantheism which Mendelssohn was far from possessing. His attitude towards Spinoza had undergone no change since in his *Philosophical Dialogues* he had almost wept over the incongruity of so good and virtuous a man falling into such grievous philosophical errors "which the vilest criminal would welcome as enabling him to indulge his worst passions with impunity." Such ethical prejudice was bound to obscure his intellectual vision.

The beginning of the trouble which did much to darken the closing years of Mendelssohn's life was a casual meeting of Lessing and F. H. Jacobi at Wolfenbüttel where Jacobi was visiting. Jacobi was a disciple of Bonnet and an intimate friend of the dyspeptic Hamann. He was an amiable fanatic and mystic, who distrusted reason and founded his philosophy on faith and feeling. All philosophic demonstration he maintained led logically and inevitably to Spinozism, that is to say Atheism and Fatalism. To avoid these we must set a limit to philosophic demonstration and acknowledge that the higher truths must be understood through a higher faculty: faith.

One day in the course of his visit Jacobi gave Lessing Goethe's poem *Prometheus* to read, saying: "As you have caused so much annoyance to others I trust this will annoy you." Lessing, however, expressed his delight with both form and ideas and still further staggered Jacobi by assuring him: "The viewpoint of this poem is my own. I no longer hold the orthodox notions about God; I no longer find them palatable. One and All. I know no more than that. If I am to call myself after any man I know of no other than Spinoza." When Jacobi had recovered his power of speech he elicited the further statement that Lessing had never revealed his views to Mendelssohn. He knew it would be useless.

It was only three years later, when Jacobi heard that Mendelssohn meant to write a sketch of Lessing, that Jacobi confided the terrible secret to a mutual friend, Elise Reimarus. Mendelssohn was not at first inclined to attach too much importance to the information. He looked upon it as a mere legendary report, an anecdote, but soon he realized that even as an anecdote the statement might do Lessing's name infinite harm. The notion that no man could possibly lead an honest and decent life unless he believed in a personal God and the immortality of the soul was so generally held even by enlightened people that calling a man a Pantheist was in Mendelssohn's time casting a slur on his moral character. It also puzzled him that Lessing should have kept this secret from him and revealed it to Jacobi of whose friendship with Lessing he had never been aware. To make sure of what had really happened he wrote to Elise Reimarus: he wanted details, the exact wording of Lessing's declaration and the circumstances in which he made it. "If," he says, "Lessing could without in any way qualifying the statement declare his adherence to the system of any man, he was either beside himself or some peculiar mood made him utter a paradox which the first serious hour would make him reject again." If, on the other hand, he had merely said that the notorious Spinoza had in many things seen further than all his critics, that there were more excellent things in his *Ethics* than in many an orthodox system of morals, then he, Mendelssohn, was ready to subscribe to that himself.

Jacobi's reply made Mendelssohn realize what he had let himself in for. Jacobi's very unusual intelligence, his profound knowledge of Spinoza combined with a disconcerting mode of composition "reminiscent of the jumping of a grasshopper" made him a particularly difficult opponent to tackle, especially for a Mendelssohn whose strength lay in sincerity of conviction, in clearness, and directness of thought rather than in nimbleness and the skilful use of metaphor. "I see clearly," he confesses to Elise Reimarus, "that I have misjudged Mr. Jacobi. I took him for a bel-esprit, only occasionally interested in philosophic matters, and I find a man who has made thinking the main business of his life, who has the strength to free himself from all leading-strings and go his own way. Of his reply which you have forwarded to me I have only understood the smallest part. At the first reading I found the progress of his ideas too strange, his imagery too dazzling and the gaps in his presentation so striking that I felt stunned and could not get my bearings. . . . I had misjudged the knight I had so insolently challenged! He raised his visor, I know my man and with all humility I pick up my glove again."

"In any case," he adds by way of comfort to his soul, "I have no intention, when I write about Lessing, to represent him either as a prophet or as a saint. . . . Whether my dearest Lessing went off to the right or to the left during the last days of his life is a matter of indifference to me. I attach little importance to what even the greatest man does or says in his last hours especially when he is as fond of sudden digressions as Lessing. What was novel and striking counted for more with him than truth and simplicity. He might even have sent for a parson if such a thing had struck him as an ingenious idea."

In the end he entreats Elise's brother to take upon his shoulders the task of unravelling the tangle he had unwittingly created. "You know the weakness of my nerves from which I have been suffering for over ten years," he says. "An effort of this kind would surely shatter my brain. The worst is that I have nothing new, nothing striking to tell these people. The old, well-known reasons, no matter how valid and convincing they may appear to me, are a laughing-stock for the sophists of our age. . . . I believe that you, my friend, have still got the strength and the energy to enter the lists against these men. As your faithful assistant and shield-bearer, I shall stand by your side, and while you bend your bow, I shall sharpen your arrows and hand them to you."

The whole letter is a pathetic groan. His despair, however, does not arise from offended vanity, for the author of *Phaedo* was the most modest of men; it arises from a galling feeling that his fighting days are over, that he is too old and weak and ill-armed to defend the cause of natural religion which was almost as sacred to him as that of Judaism itself, indeed lay at the very foundation of Judaism. For nine months he delayed a reply to Jacobi's explicit statement and then he expressed his regret that he was unable to understand many passages in Jacobi's letter. He told him that for the moment he had given up the idea of writing about Lessing but he enclosed a brief statement of objections to Spinozism. Before long a somewhat boorish reply (the gentle Mendelssohn called it German frankness) came from Jacobi enclosing a defence of the consistency of Spinozism and there for a time the matter rested. The more Jacobi had written the less Mendelssohn had understood. In mental equipment, standpoint and method the two contestants were too far apart ever to reach a common ground and Mendelssohn felt they were entertaining each other like the stork and the fox in the fable, the stork serving the food in deep flagons and the fox in shallow dishes. The host in each case looked after his own mouth only and let his guest starve.

It was not until the autumn of 1785, when Mendelssohn's *Morning Hours* had just appeared, that Jacobi resumed the fight by publishing *On the Doctrine of Spinoza* in which he sets out to prove that Spinozism is Atheism, that the Kabbalistic philosophy is nothing but undeveloped or confused Spinozism, that the philosophy of Leibnitz and Wolff is not less fatalistic than that of Spinoza and carries a resolute thinker to the very principles of Spinoza, that every demonstrative method ends in Fatalism, that the keystone (*Element*) of all human knowledge and activity is belief or faith (*Glaube*). It was a characteristically tactless act on the part of the author, for the book contained among other things the whole of his correspondence with Elise Reimarus and Mendelssohn on the subject of Lessing's supposed Pantheism. The publication of Mendelssohn's letters was as unexpected as it was unauthorized and the betrayal of the secret confided to Jacobi affected Mendelssohn most painfully.

In spite of the emphatic assurances of Mendelssohn in his letters that Lessing's supposed profession of Pantheism had no significance whatever we are not surprised to find him now in a state of morbid agitation. The case against Lessing had in Mendelssohn's eyes assumed a desperately serious aspect as the result of Jacobi's latest exposition of Spinozism. The Spinozist Lessing was now inevitably an atheist and a fatalist. Yet according to Mendelssohn's *Jerusalem* the belief in a personal God was the only foundation of virtue. In his pleas for the freedom of thought and the non-interference of the state with religious and philosophical opinion he had specifically excepted Atheism which he bracketed with Epicurism as undermining the foundations of civilized society. Moreover Jacobi's challenge had excited phenomenal interest throughout Germany. Many to whom Spinoza had hitherto been a mere name began to study his philosophy undeterred by the awful danger of which Jacobi warned them. Goethe's interest in Pantheism dates from that time. It is rather amusing to reflect that in combating Spinozism Jacobi probably did more to spread pantheistic views than any champion of that philosophy.

Ethically Jacobi appears, of course, in an unenviable light. He had published private letters without the consent of the writers. He had betrayed, not only to Mendelssohn but to the whole world, Lessing's confidential statement regarding convictions of which Mendelssohn had so long been mercifully kept in ignorance. He had in the eyes of many irretrievably damaged the reputation of a man who could no longer defend himself. We can understand Mendelssohn's indignation. A reply to Jacobi's challenge seemed urgently called for. For the last time he set his pen on paper to write the pathetic *To the Friends of Lessing* (An die Freunde Lessings).

XXVI

IN DEFENCE OF LESSING

Mendelssohn's defence could not possibly be a full reply to all the theses set up by Jacobi. There was enough there to occupy a man's time for a whole year. He contents himself with a brief statement which is more remarkable for the generosity of the motive which prompted it than for its conclusiveness. It was clearly written in a great hurry and under the stress of strong emotion. On one page he protests against the suggestion that Lessing was a hypocrite and a blasphemer, on the next he will ask: "Supposing he was a Spinozist, what have speculative doctrines got to do with the man himself? Who would not be glad to have had Spinoza himself for a friend however much of a Spinozist he may have been? Who would refuse to do justice to the genius and the excellent character of Spinoza?" We might almost conclude that not Spinozism itself is what he objects to but Spinozism kept secret. Possibly, he suggests, Lessing was an adherent of the refined form of Spinozism which is not at all antagonistic to Judaism. "Spinoza himself," he adds somewhat questionably, "in spite of his speculative views could have remained an orthodox Jew, had he not in other writings combated genuine Judaism and thus have left the law." As he cannot altogether deny the substantial accuracy of Jacobi's account of Lessing's remarks, he offers the startling explanation that Jacobi, seeing in Lessing a man of unstable principles who could champion Theism one day, Atheism the next and the day after perhaps even superstition resolved to cure him of this confusion of spirit. "As a skilful physician he ventured at first to aggravate the disease in order to cure it all the more certainly. He led Lessing further and further into the mazes of Spinozism, making him lose himself among the thorny hedges of Pantheism in order to render all the more attractive the only way out he will then show him. This exit as we now clearly perceive is a retreat under the banner of faith. . . . In that manner Lessing was to be brought back to the way of truth from which he had made him stray."

According to Mendelssohn Lessing treated the whole thing as a joke, let Jacobi commit himself up to the neck and enjoyed himself hugely. Having failed to convert Lessing Jacobi thought of Mendelssohn as just as much in need of philosophical salvation by faith and possibly less hard to convince than Lessing. So he used the Lessing confession as a cunning innuendo. It is, of course, not very clear why he should have looked upon the stiff-necked hero of the Mendelssohn-Lavater controversy as an easy mark, but the hypothesis gives Mendelssohn an opportunity to reaffirm his unalterable allegiance to Judaism, a hint to Jacobi that this attempt at conversion would meet with the same failure as a similar effort made by Lavater in 1769.

The remainder of *To the Friends of Lessing* is a reprint of the statement of the objections to Spinozism he had sent Jacobi the preceding year. He had understood Jacobi's disquisitions very imperfectly, his supplementary explanations still less. So further discussion was unprofitable and humiliating. "I know as little," he says, "what to make of Herr Jacobi's practical principles as of his theoretical. In these circumstances it would be better for us to part. Let him return to the faith of his fathers and by the victorious power of faith subdue heavy-mouthed reason, let him defeat any doubts that might arise by authorities and dictatorial pronunciamentos. Let him bless and seal his filial return with words from the pious and angelic lips of Lavater. I, on the other hand, shall persist in my Jewish unbelief. Not crediting any mortal man with angelic lips I should not care to be dependent even on the authority of an archangel when eternal truths are under discussion on which the happiness of mankind is founded. I have to stand on my own feet or fall. Or rather, as according to Herr Jacobi, we are all born in the faith of my fathers which is not a faith in doctrines and opinions, but confidence and trust in the attributes of God. I have unlimited confidence in the omnipotence of God to grant to human beings the power to apprehend without authorities truths on which their happiness depends, and I have the childlike trust in his mercy to have granted this power to me also. . . . I believe that I have found these truths and that anyone can find them who seeks with his eyes open and does not stand in his own light."

"As for our friend Lessing, his lot is after all not quite so hard as might have been expected at first. Herr Jacobi assigns to him a society in which he will not be too unhappy. . . . The philosophy of Leibnitz and Wolff is to his mind no less fatalistic than that of Spinoza and leads the resolute thinker to the principles of the latter. Every mode of demonstration he says ends in fatalism. The spirit of Lessing who used to find such pleasure in the intercourse· with these reprobates need not fear being bored by their society. Let him, therefore, return pacified to the tranquil dwellings of peace, to the arms of the men who like him have trodden the path of demonstration and like him have trusted their reason."

Mendelssohn's last work, *To the Friends of Lessing,* was not published during his lifetime. In the evening of the thirty-first of December, 1785, he had rushed the manuscript to the publishers. He complained of pain when he returned. Imagining it was a simple cold he did not send for the doctor who, however, heard of Mendelssohn's illness and called on the second of January, but could do little. In the morning of the fourth he died suddenly. Opposite the sofa on which he lay stood the bust of Lessing for whose memory he had fought so valiantly to the end.

The grief the news of his death evoked throughout the whole of Germany and the public demonstration of sympathy shown on the occasion of his funeral mark a turning-point in the history of Jewish-Christian relations in Germany. Jews as well as Christians of all shades escorted his remains to the cemetery and the loss to his friends and to the world in general was felt to be irreparable.

"Lessing died," said one of the Berlin newspapers, "when he had finished *Nathan,* had dispelled the night of superstition and shown God to mortals in his purest and sublimest light. His friend died after devoting his last thoughts to the most exalted theme of human thought, the demonstration of the existence of this Deity in whose contemplation they now found their happiness."

Mendelssohn left behind him three sons and two daughters. His eldest son Joseph, besides writing a book on Rossetti's interpretation of Dante, founded along with his brother Abraham a well-known Berlin banking-house. The younger son Nathan was an excellent engineer and entered the service of the state. The eldest daughter Dorothea, one of the best known intellectuals of the period and the heroine of Schlegel's notorious *Lucinde,* ultimately became the wife of Friedrich Schlegel, one of the leaders of the Romantic Movement. Her younger sister Henriette became governess in the family of the French Field-marshal Sébastiani. Among Mendelssohn's grand-children we find Joseph's son Georg Benjamin, professor in the University of Bonn and editor of his grandfather's works as well as the two sons of Dorothea by a first marriage, the eminent painters Johann and Philipp Veit, and Abraham's son, the composer Felix Mendelssohn-Bartholdy.

It is interesting to reflect that in ancient Sparta the sickly cripple would have been exposed as a child and left to die of starvation, while the fanatics of modern eugenics would not have allowed him to marry.

MENDELSSOHN THE CRITIC, PHILOSOPHER AND "REFORMER"

What is Mendelssohn's place in philosophy, literature and the emancipation of his people?

One might imagine that, a century and a half having elapsed since his death, some kind of agreement might have been reached regarding his standing. This is not so. We still meet with a bewildering variety of judgments ranging from contemptuous silence to fulsome praise bordering on mendacity. While the former may no doubt be to some extent the natural reaction to the latter, the oblivion into which a man so prominent in his own time has sunk must be accounted for in some other way. The fact that he was a Jew, while it may explain Jewish panegyrics, has probably very little to do with the regrettable fading of the memory of the man. The explanation is rather to be sought in the purely relative value, the purely historical importance of many of his most famous works, the imperfection of others due to the obvious gaps in his equipment, his want of historic sense and the uncritical reliance he places on such predecessors as Leibnitz and Wolff whose results he looks upon as almost indisputable. The proofs he marshals in his *Phaedo* for the immortality of the soul have lost their cogency for us. His demonstration of the existence of God was even more unfortunate: it was shown to be worthless four years before it saw the light of day and a great deal of what he has written about Spinoza is vitiated by the author's conviction that any result but the one he ultimately attains would be fraught with disaster to virtue and the happiness of mankind.

Mendelssohn's appearance as a contemporary of giants like Lessing in literary criticism and Kant in philosophy has no doubt also tended to detract from the importance of the part he plays. The light of even a greater man than Mendelssohn would have been dimmed by the dazzling effulgence of such stars of the first magnitude. His friendship, too, with Lessing, was not an unmixed blessing for his fame. In such dangerous juxtaposition he soon lost all claim to a renown of his own and finally became known as just "Lessing's friend."

Mendelssohn's philosophic ambition was as unpretentious as the man himself. "I have never dreamt," he says, "of marking an epoch in philosophy or of becoming famous through a system of my own. Where I see a trodden path before me I do not seek to make a new one. When my predecessors have fixed the meaning of a word why should I not accept it? When they have dragged a truth to light why should I pretend that I did not know it? The re-proach of sectarianism does not deter me from ac-cepting with a grateful heart anything useful I find in them." But if he has not given us a system of his own he at least enjoys the distinction of having been by far the clearest and the most attractive ex-ponent of the philosophy of the Enlightenment with which he had identified himself.

He was indeed the most consistent disciple of that school of thought. The aim and object of all his philosophizing was not so much the quest of truth as the happiness of mankind. When he sought truth it was mainly such truth as would contribute to such happiness, which thus often came very near being made the sole test of truth. "It delights me some-times," says Mendelssohn, "to consider that every idea from which humanity might derive comfort and advantage, if it were true, becomes for that very reason highly probable." The immortality of the soul was thus highly probable in Mendelssohn's eyes even before he set to work to inquire into the truth of it. With such a naïve criterion Mendelssohn could not, except by the merest accident, obtain any results of permanent philosophical value. When in a letter to Kant Mendelssohn, lamenting the time he had wasted in fruitless, because unguided, attempts to attain to the true and the beautiful, exclaims: "Oh, that before my twentieth year I had had a Kant for my friend!" we do not share his confidence that he would have been any different as a philosopher. The orthodox Jew and the iconoclast Kant would have parted company long before the former reached the point where he could write to Elise Reimarus: "I was very pleased to learn that your brother does not think very kindly of the *Critique of Pure Reason* which I confess I do not understand. . . . I am happy to think I am not missing much if I depart without understanding this work."

Mendelssohn nevertheless performed an important function by greatly stimulating a general interest in philosophical questions among all people with any pretence of culture. The task of popularization was rendered possible by Mendelssohn using German as Wolff had done before him. The almost exclusive use of Latin or French by German scholars had at one time gone so far that Leibnitz expressed the fear that "soon German would vanish from Germany as Anglo-Saxon had vanished from England." But if to Wolff belongs the merit of having been the first German philosopher to write his works in German Mendelssohn went a great deal further than Wolff. The dry philosophical jargon of his predecessor became in his hands a language such as very few Germans had written before him. Kant, who could speak feelingly of this matter, his own style being abominable, said of Mendelssohn's: "One should as little expect to see one and the same style in all writers as the same bark on all trees. Still, Mendelssohn's mode of writing seems to me the best suited for philosophy. It is so free from all striving after dazzling ornamentation and yet so elegant, so ingenious and yet so clear. It aims so little at moving the reader by mere show and is yet so impressive. If the muse of philosophy were to choose a language, this is the one she would choose." If his philosophical works have lost what scientific value his contemporaries attached to them, some of them, particularly *Phaedo,* we still treasure as unique models of style. In any case modern destructive criticism centres on the main argument of his works and leaves untouched many of the subsidiary and incidental portions which are often very stimulating and furnish delightful reading.

In literature Mendelssohn's work was purely critical. He possessed no creative talent whatever. On his criticism he brought to bear precisely the same qualities as on his philosophical work: clearness, a sense of order, freedom from prejudice combined with a wonderfully fresh and fascinating style. Unfortunately the excessive importance he attaches to reason, the encouragement of virtue and the bringing about of what he conceives to be the happiness of mankind narrow the range of his literary appreciation. His criterion of the excellence of poetry is so incompatible with the true nature and function of poetry as to be in many cases perfectly useless. Poetry does not interest him except when it is used to convey truth and, even then, it had, of course, to be the truth as he knew it. It even happens that when his eye lights on real poetry he does not know what to do with it. Of Goethe's magnificent *Prometheus* he says in one place that it is "a pitiable performance, crammed with quixotic matter." In another place, he imagines that he has discovered its esoteric meaning. "I liked the poem *Prometheus*," he says. "It is a very good persiflage! Nothing can show the so-called Spinozist system in all its nakedness in a more telling manner. Its gaps never strike one more forcibly than when it is reduced to common sense by the aid of poetry."

While in philosophy Mendelssohn owes little to Lessing, some of his main literary ideas are Lessing's. We often distinctly hear the voice of the master. Together they pricked many a contemporary bubble and a number of Mendelssohn's judgments have the finality of Lessing's, though others for the reasons given above have not been sustained by posterity. Mendelssohn was Lessing's ablest lieutenant in his war on shams and mediocrities and, in his inauguration of the new school of criticism which had in view the interests of the reader rather than those of the author, aimed at telling the reader the truth about the work reviewed and enabled him to form his own judgment. The old school disdainfully neglected the reader, contented itself with dispensing literary patronage or condemning to the whipping-post, overwhelming the author with extravagant adulation or pelting him with gross insults.

Mendelssohn's knowledge of literature seems astounding especially if we take into account that his literary criticism falls mainly into the few years between 1756 and 1765 and that his duties of bookkeeper to Bernhard's silk factory absorbed his best energies during the greater part of the day so that his varied and extensive reading had to be done before seven in the morning or late in the afternoon or the evening.

In view of the philosophical bent of his mind, Mendelssohn could not fail to be interested in aesthetics. From the very beginning of his career he had indeed been attracted by the study of the fundamental questions of the science. His achievements along this line have not always received the appreciation or even the notice they deserve. The historians of aesthetics neglect him almost entirely. On the other hand, there is no justification for overstating his achievements by saying that "Mendelssohn laid the foundations of German aesthetics." [1] These foundations were laid by Alexander Baumgarten who published his first work on the subject in 1750 and had been lecturing on it for some years previously. Mendelssohn made, however, a number of minor contributions, the most interesting being a suggestion which probably gave rise to one of the

[1] Israel Cohen, *Jewish Life in Modern Times.*

most fundamental works on aesthetics, Lessing's *Laokoon*.

There is no doubt that it was he who started the whole *Laokoon* discussion in a letter addressed to Lessing in December 1756. A little later in his *Main Principles of the Fine Arts and Sciences* (Hauptgrundzüge der schönen Künste und Wissenschaften) he was the first to point out the fundamental difference between the art of poetry and the plastic arts with regard to their means of expression and therefore the things to be expressed by them. Lessing's *Laokoon* is built up on this fundamental distinction and the result of Lessing's lucid and convincing exposition dealt the deathblow to the mischievous superstition that "painting is dumb poetry and poetry speaking painting," a confusion of thought which was responsible for the profusion of allegorical painting and descriptive poetry of Lessing's time. On the other hand, it is equally true that it was Lessing, not Mendelssohn, who worked out all the logical consequences of Mendelssohn's suggestion and particularly who formulated the law which is the theme of *Laokoon*. Mendelssohn was so far from suspecting the full bearing of his suggestion that, towards the end of the same essay in which he made it, he maintains that "even the subtlest thoughts, the most abstract ideas can be expressed on the painter's canvas." He did not notice the flat contradiction of the principle he had laid down shortly before.

Lessing's creative work was in no way influenced by his friend. That Lessing modelled his Nathan on Mendelssohn is a myth due to a superficial acquaintance with Lessing or Mendelssohn or Nathan or all three. Obviously Lessing must often have thought of his Jewish friend during the composition of *Nathan the Wise* but the result was nevertheless that ethically and intellectually Nathan is preeminently Lessing himself. The difference between Mendelssohn and Nathan is abysmal. Intellectually Mendelssohn is Nathan's inferior, ethically he towers above him. Both facts are brought out by their conduct in analogous experiences. The astute Nathan extricates himself from the embarrassing situation created by the Sultan's question regarding the best religion by a poetic quibble. The guileless Mendelssohn's answer to a similar question put by Lavater has something of the noble grandeur of Luther's: *Hier stehe ich, ich kann nicht anders.* "Of the essentials of my religion," he answered, "I feel as firmly, as irrefutably assured as you can be of yours, and I declare before God that I shall adhere to my principles as long as my whole soul does not change in character."

In other respects it is less easy to determine how much Mendelssohn owed to Lessing and how much Lessing owed to Mendelssohn. With regard to Mendelssohn's own view of this question as expressed in the letter he wrote to Lessing's brother shortly after Lessing's death liberal allowance has, of course, to be made for the circumstances in which it was written. One thing is certain, that the title "the friend of Lessing," which is often the only thing people seem to know about Mendelssohn, presents rather a mean and one-sided view of the case. After all, Lessing was also "the friend of Mendelssohn." Their correspondence which in point of importance is duplicated in German Literature only by that between Goethe and Schiller furnishes abundant proof that the help and inspiration was mutual. They were admirably fitted to work together. They were agreed, at first at least, on fundamentals, particularly the love of truth and their duty to seek it. They showed the same freedom from conceit. They took delight in quickly and accurately establishing differences and defining ideas, an important function of the literary critic at a time when confusion reigned with regard to some of the most elementary working notions.

On the other hand, they differed in their method of approaching the problem of truth. Lessing, having serious misgivings about the possibility of attaining truth, contented himself with "hunting error out of its lair, dragging it into the light of day, calling it to account and striking it with the sharpest of his weapons." [2] The gentle Mendelssohn whose nature shrank from polemics of all kinds had a tender spot in his heart even for error if it was in

[2] J. Auerbach, *Moses Mendelssohn und das Judentum.*

any way connected with some important truth. It was by spreading the truth that he tried to overcome error. That truth was attainable he firmly believed. Had he not shown to the satisfaction of the Berlin Academy that even metaphysical truth was attainable with something approaching mathematical certainty? Moreover, he looked upon the true and the good as so intimately connected that non-attainment of the one would necessarily involve the non-attainment of the other. This would lead to a moral cataclysm the very possibility of which was precluded by the doctrine of the pre-established harmony of the universe, one of Mendelssohn's fundamental beliefs.

At first it was no doubt Lessing who gave and Mendelssohn who received: the introduction to the literary society of Berlin invaluable and indispensable in the case of a Jew, the inspiration and encouragement in his first literary and philosophical essays. Lessing's style then was the model on which he formed his own, so much so that in his earlier works there are definitions, demonstrations, whole paragraphs and even pages that might have been written by Lessing. Later on he developed a style which was entirely his own, more elegant, graceful and pleasing than Lessing's, without, however, the latter's picturesqueness, boldness and passionate fervour.

Gradually Mendelssohn emancipated himself not

only with regard to style but also, and perhaps
mainly, with regard to ideas and interests. His adverse criticism of Lessing's *Education of the Human Race* and his attitude towards the publication
of the *Reimarus Fragments* along with the desultory
character of their correspondence from 1762 until
Lessing's death showed how seriously they had
drifted apart. The difference of mental and cultural
background, no longer veiled by the optimism of
their younger years, became more and more marked.
Every fibre in Lessing was modern, ultra-modern.
In many ways he was almost a century ahead of his
time. He was cosmopolitan to the finger-tips. He
was ever clearly and serenely conscious of the full
significance and the logical consequences of every
word he wrote. This unity of character, this freedom of thought and action was wanting in Mendelssohn, who was only one half modern, while the other
half was deeply rooted in philosophical and cultural
traditions of the past.

Lessing and Mendelssohn were admirably matched
travelling companions during the first part of their
journey, but soon Lessing's pace became distressing to his more heavily-burdened comrade. He left
him far behind and at the end we see Mendelssohn
unable to feel at home in the perilous regions towards
which the daring Lessing was heading his course,
standing still and casting back wistful glances at the
pleasant regions of an all-good and an all-wise God,

a pre-established harmony, and a modest allowance of state interference with religious and philosophical opinion.

What part did such a man play in the spiritual, cultural and political emancipation of the Jews? It used to be the fashion to picture him as the reformer and emancipator of Judaism. In many ways he was really unfitted to play such a part. His whole nature, physical and mental, shrank from the task, nor had he any desire to put himself forward in any such capacity. He abominated polemics and had nothing of the ruthlessness, the brutal want of consideration for other people's feelings which are inseparable from the true reformer's mentality. In a letter to Elise Reimarus, dated 21st. Sept., 1784, he says: "Even though I had the power to destroy every prejudice with a single stroke of the pen I should carefully refrain from doing so." As already stated he did not object to error if it could be shown to be of a useful type or to be connected with what he conceived to be good for the happiness of mankind. He was particularly averse to appearing as the champion of the Jewish cause. He had no faith whatever in active interference, in militant propaganda, holding that such action came most effectively from Christians. He has sometimes even been accused of want of sympathy where Jewish interests were concerned. It is true he never dreamt of making any effort to agitate for a general improvement of the civil status of the Jews and that, through surely excessive fear of arousing the prejudices of the Christian authorities, he weakly refrained from suggesting changes in the wording of the offensive and degrading oath imposed upon Jews when giving evidence in courts of law. So it is all the more to his credit that on several occasions he overcame his natural timidity and showed that he could act energetically in the interest of his oppressed coreligionists when it was a question of setting right a definite individual act of injustice or tyranny.

Mendelssohn was as little a religious as he was a political or a social reformer. If anyone had suggested to him that he should reform Judaism, the suggestion would have left him breathless. He saw nothing to reform in Judaism: the metaphysical portion was guaranteed by reason, and the law by revelation. He was and remained to his dying day an orthodox Jew obeying all the laws of conduct of his religion. He tells us that so far from finding the law irksome he positively enjoyed carrying it out to the last detail.

A point in which he differed from probably many Jews was the origin of the metaphysical portion of the Jewish faith: the existence of God as the creator of the universe, the judge of good and evil and the author of the moral law. These beliefs while he held them firmly, we owed, he said, to our unaided reason. The need for revelation he saw only in the case of the elaborate ceremonial law. While such an attitude in no way impaired his orthodoxy, i. e. if the degree of a man's orthodoxy is determined by the number of dogmas he holds, his distinction between the rational and the revealed portion of the Scriptures was a dangerous one to make. It did away with the divine self-revelation and the divine authority of the moral law, as distinct from the civil law of the Ten Commandments. The only divine portion left was an inexplicable ceremonial comparable to the "court ceremonial of an oriental despot" [3] and incumbent on Jews only. Relegating a revealed Deity to a corner in the Old Testament seemed to undermine the authority of that record and, by the very juxtaposition of revealed and non-revealed portions, to weaken the foundations of the ceremonial law itself. In any case, leaving the metaphysical portion of religion at the mercy of reason has always proved a perilous venture. Reason is much harder to satisfy than faith, and the discovery of any flaw in the argument is liable to bring the whole edifice crashing to the ground.

There have been times in Jewish history when this rationalist attitude might have been taken up by a leader in Israel without danger to the religious morale of the people. Orthodox contról was easy in the seclusion of the ghetto, it became impossible when, fol-

[3] Steinheim, *Moses Mendelssohn und seine Schule.*

lowing the example set by Mendelssohn and others, Jew and Gentile began to mingle. The danger was, of course, vastly increased by Mendelssohn's standing among Jews and Gentiles, by the lure of his clear and attractive style, the universal popularity of his writings and by his extraordinary personality which enabled him without concealment or hypocrisy to be a Jew to the Jews and yet to appear to Christians divested of all the characteristics which in fact or fiction had made the Jew an object of contempt and hatred. "His character and conduct," says Kayserling, "were a disavowal of all the objectionable qualities ascribed to the Jews: the cringing servility, the arrogance, obtrusiveness, ignorance, wrongheadedness, and want of tact."

Was there not another danger lurking in this insistence on the ceremonial law as the only revealed portion of the Old Testament? "Evasions demoralize, and in a ceremonial religion whose followers have to maintain old customs in new environments evasions seem inevitable. The effect of this on the Jewish character has always been bad." [4] There had been evasions at all times, even in ghetto times, but now these escapes from restraint degenerated into a rout. Other Jews beside Mendelssohn, some encouraged by his example and the success and fame he had achieved, others independently, sought closer contact with their environment either as a matter of

---

[4] I. Abrahams, *Jewish Life in the Middle Ages.*

personal predilection or because they looked upon such contact as the only solution for Judaism as a civilizing force. Some of these deserters were perhaps less strong than Mendelssohn, more prone to yield to the temptation of material and social advantages held out as a reward to those who ceased to be *Stockjuden,* others perhaps were less blind to the logical inconsistency of Mendelssohn's philosophical attitude. For one man like Mendelssohn who managed to harmonize within himself the hopelessly conflicting claims of the old Judaism and the new culture there were hundreds of others who soon gave up the struggle in despair. Chodowiecki's letter to the Countess von Solms-Laubach shows with what rapidity this demoralization had gone apace. "The Jews of Berlin," he wrote in 1783, "are no longer concerned with any kind of ritual; they buy and sell on Saturdays, eat all forbidden foods, keep no fast days. Only the lower classes are still orthodox."

This state of things was the product of a variety of factors. We have in the first place the sudden and radical change of the philosophic, social and economic outlook of the eighteenth century of which men like Mendelssohn were as much an effect as they were a cause. The rationalist movement tended to efface racial, religious and social distinctions, discouraged exclusiveness of all kinds and, incidentally, created an atmosphere of religious indifference, which for the first time allowed the Jew to cease being a Jew without having to become a Christian. Further, with the rise of industrialism the Jewish capitalist became a person of far greater importance than he had ever been and the possession of wealth and brains tended more and more to take the place of noble birth, purity of racial descent and ardour of religious faith as a criterion of respectability.

There is one reform due to Mendelssohn of which we may say that its author really willed it as a reform and was clearly aware of some of the cultural changes it would bring about, his German translation of the Pentateuch and the Psalms. It resulted in a form of emancipation which was not a mere drifting away from the restraint of old beliefs and traditions. It rather put a stop to the drifting, at least for a time, by leading the people back to the fountainhead of their religion which had become unintelligible in its original Hebrew. At the same time by a strange paradox it also proved the path which led from exclusive Judaism to inclusion in German nationality. With the substitution of German for the imperfectly understood Hebrew and the uncultural Yiddish, the knowledge of which led nowhere, new educational ideals could oust the worn-out shibboleths of the ghetto. The champions of Jewish exclusiveness might protest vehemently against the perils threatening the Chosen People from assimilation and absorption. Yet assimilation, at least, was inevitable. It is a generally observed fact that a lower form of culture surrounded by a higher can keep itself intact only on condition of being surrounded by a wall as the Jews literally were in ghetto times. As soon as free contact and community of interests are established, nothing short of a miracle can prevent the assimilation of the lower to the higher.

It is interesting and at the same time pathetic to see how Mendelssohn who never asked for anything more for his people than equal opportunities and would even have been satisfied with the bare freedom from humiliating and irritating oppression should have been instrumental in facilitating this assimilation which to him was anathema. Had he foreseen such a result he would rather have cut off his right hand than pen a single word that might tend towards such disaster." He would rather have continued to suffer with his people believing that he was thereby fulfilling the purpose of God who would surely some day reward them for what they had suffered for his sake." He would have considered the realization of his dream of the lion lying down with the lamb bought at too dear a price.

It is, of course, absurd to set down the Jewish Reform Movement entirely to Mendelssohn's account. He was only a wheel within the complicated machinery of civilization. He was not merely driving but being driven. At most, he was like every leader of a people the interpreter of the yearnings and im-

pulses around him. These were all for freedom and
equal opportunities. Jewish exclusiveness in its
various manifestations, its claim of racial superiority, its rigid adherence to practices incompatible
with modern life and its separate language was the
main obstacle. Yet all these were the very foundation of the national cohesion and solidarity of the
Jewish people. By his taboo of Yiddish, the only
separate language the Jews knew, Mendelssohn shat-
tered one of the pillars of Jewish national solidarity
and by his rationalistic philosophy he seriously
threatened another, thereby clearing the way towards
a much fuller emancipation than he had ever con-
templated.

Obviously the reserved and shrinking Mendelssohn thus accomplished more than any militant
propagandist could have achieved at a time which
was not ripe for such propaganda. If he was unfitted to be a reformer in the popular sense of the
word, he was nevertheless peculiarly suited to the
part he played in the cultural movement of the second
half of the eighteenth century. Though timid almost
to the verge of cowardice where his people as a whole
was concerned, he was magnificently courageous
where his own personal convictions were at stake.
None of his contemporaries, whether Jew or Gentile,
has stood up more bravely in defence of the right of
private judgment. When his duty as a critic required
it, he openly passed censure on what he held to be the

pernicious philosophical views of the autocratic King of Prussia. Without flinching he picked up the glove thrown down by Lavater and plunged into a controversy fraught with the greatest danger to himself, and with his German translation of the Pentateuch he defied the whole of orthodox Jewry. With all his yearning for freedom he had the perspicacity to see that in the fight for emancipation the first battle would have to be waged within the precincts of the spiritual ghetto of the Jews and that the cultural level of his coreligionists would have to be raised enormously before there could be any thought of recognition of the Jews as German citizens. He stood out as a splendid example of what character, culture and intellectual eminence can do to overcome inveterate prejudice and to wrest the recognition of equality from a hostile environment.

But, though we may say that with Mendelssohn the Jew became a participant in the surrounding German culture and, very soon, a generous and even prolific contributor to it, the process of nationalizing the Jewish alien was desperately slow and is even now, after the lapse of a hundred and fifty years, far from being completed. The Jew who was content to drift away from the religion and the culture of his fathers presented, of course, no problem. He was absorbed. But the Jew who attempted what a Mendelssohn succeeded in doing, reconciling within himself two antagonistic cultural backgrounds, the ancient Jewish and the modern German, had and still has a rough road to travel. The welcome extended to him is at best not very cordial. In times of nationalistic hysteria or economic depression he may even provoke active hostility and when he reacts, perhaps very naturally, by seeking comfort in the separate nationalism of the Zionist movement, he seems to surrender, bound hand and foot, to his chauvinistic detractors, who ask for nothing better than such a frank confession of separate national aspirations.

The tragic feature of the Jewish problem is that every remedy offered, from Mendelssohn to Herzl, while relieving the situation in one direction, invariably complicates it in another.

BIBLIOGRAHPY

ABRAHAMS, I., *Jewish Life in the Middle Ages,* Philadelphia, 1911.

AUERBACH, J., "Moses Mendelssohn und das Judenthum," *Zeitschrift für die Geschichte des Judenthums,* 1887.

BERLINER, A., *Aus dem Leben der deutschen Juden im Mittelalter.* Berlin, 1900.

BERTHOLET, A., *Kulturgeschichte Israels.* Göttingen, 1919.

CAHN, N., *Moses Mendelssohns Moralphilosophie.* Giessen.

COHEN, B., *Ueber die Erkenntnislehre Moses Mendelssohns.* Giessen, 1921.

COHEN, I., *Jewish Life in Modern Times.* London, 1914.

DUSCHENES, F., *Gedächtnisrede.* Prag, 1886.

FISHBERG, M., *The Jews.* London, 1911.

FRANKL, F. P., "Erbauungs-und Unterhaltungslektüre unserer Altvordern," *Monatsschrift für Geschichte und Wissenschaft des Judenthums,* 1885.

FROMER, J., *Vom Ghetto zur modernen Kultur.* Charlottenburg, 1906.

GEIGER, L., *Geschichte der Juden in Berlin.* Berlin, 1871.

GEIGER, L., *Vor hundert Jahren.*

GOLDHAMMER, L., *Die Psychologie Moses Mendelssohns.* Wien, 1886.

214 *BIBLIOGRAPHY*

GOLDSTEIN, L., *Die Bedeutung Moses Mendelssohns für die Entwickelung der ästhetischen Kritik und Theorie in Deutschland*. Königsberg i Pr.

GOLDSTEIN, L., *Moses Mendelssohn und die deutsche Aesthetik*. Königsberg, 1904.

GLÜCKEL VON HAMELN, *Denkwürdigkeiten*. Berlin, 1918.

GRAETZ, *History of the Jews*. Philadelphia, 1891–98.

GÜDEMANN, M., *Geschichte des Erziehungswesens und der Kultur der Juden*. Wien, 1880.

HAROWITZ, J., *Der Toleranzgedanke in der deutschen Literatur zur Zeit Moses Mendelssohns*. Stuttgart, 1914.

HERZBERG, I., *Moses Mendelssohn, ein Lebensbild*. Leipzig.

VON HARTMANN, E., *Das Judenthum in Gegenwart und Zukunft*. Leipzig, 1885.

ISAACS, A. S., *Step by Step*. Philadelphia, 1911.

JACOBS, J., *Jewish Statistics*. London, 1891.

JELLINEK, A., *Der jüdische Stamm. Wien*, 1869.

JOËL, M., *Religiöser Vortrag*. Breslau, 1886.

KANNGIESSER, G., *Die Stellung Mendelssohns in der Geschichte der Aesthetik*. Frankfurt-am-Main, 1868.

KARPELES, G., *Jews and Judaism*. Philadelphia, 1905.

KARPELES, G., *Jewish Literature and other Essays*. Philadelphia, 1911.

KAYSERLING, M., *Moses Mendelssohn. Sein Leben und seine Werke*. Leipzig, 1865.

KAYSERLING, M., *Moses Mendelssohn; Ungedrucktes und Unbekanntes von ihm und über ihn*. Leipzig, 1883.

KAYSERLING, M., *Moses Mendelssohns philosophische und religiöse Grundsätze mit Hinblick auf Lessing.* Leipzig, 1856.
KISSELHOFF, S., *Das jüdische Volkslied.* Berlin, 1913.
KOHUT, A., *Moses Mendelssohn und seine Familie.* Dresden, 1886.
KÖLBELE, J. B., *Zweytes Schreiben an Herrn Moses Mendelssohn.* Frankfurt-am-Main, 1770.

LANDAU, H. J., *Moses Mendelssohn; eine Monographie.* Prag, 1886.
LAZARUS, M., *Ethik des Judenthums.* Frankfurt-am-Main, 1898.
LEROY-BEAULIEU, A., *Israel Among the Nations.* New York, 1895.

MAIMON, S., *Autobiography* (transl.) London, 1888.
MARCUS, S., *Die Paedagogik des israelitischen Volkes.* Wien, 1877.
MENDELSSOHNS WERKE. Leipzig, 1843.
MUNCKER, F., "Moses Mendelssohn und die deutsche Literatur," *Zeitschrift für Geschichte des Judenthums in Deutschland.* Volume I.

PHILIPPSON, D., *The Reform Movement in Judaism.* New York, 1907.
PINÈS, M., *Histoire de la Littérature judéo-allemande.* Paris, 1900.

Resultate der Jacobischen und Mendelssohnschen Philosophie; kritisch untersucht von einem Freiwilligen. Leipzig, 1786.
RIPLEY, W. Z., *Races of Europe.* New York, 1899.
RITTER, I. H., *Mendelssohn und Lessing.* Berlin.
RÖNNE und SIMON, *Verhältnisse der Juden des preussischen Staates.* Breslau, 1843.

RUPPIN, A., *The Jews of To-day*. New York, 1913.

SAMTER, N., *Judentaufen in 19ten. Jahrhundert*. Berlin, 1906.

SANDER, D., *Die Religionsphilosophie Moses Mendelssohns*. Breslau, 1894.

SCHECHTER, S., *Studies in Judaism*. Philadelphia, 1911.

SCHOLZ, H., *Die Hauptschriften zum Pantheismusstreit zwischen Jacobi und Mendelssohn*. Berlin, 1916.

SCHREIBER, E., *Moses Mendelssohns Verdienste um die deutsche Nation*. Zürich, 1880.

SCHULZ, J. H., *Der entlarvte Moses Mendelssohn*. Amsterdam, 1786.

SCHÜTZ, F. W. (von), *Leben und Meinungen Moses Mendelssohns*. Hamburg, 1787.

SLOUSCHZ, N., *Renascence of Hebrew Literature*. Philadelphia, 1909.

SOMBART, W., *The Jews and Modern Capitalism*. New York, 1913.

SPANIER-MAGDEBURG, M., *Moses Mendelssohn als Pädagog*. Eisenach, 1898.

DR. STEINHEIM, *Moses Mendelssohn und seine Schule*. Hamburg, 1840.

STEINHEIM, S. L., M. M. Büdinger's *Lebensbeschreibung*. Altona, 1844.

STRASSBURGER, B., *Geschichte der Erziehung und des Unterrichts bei den Israeliten*. Stuttgart, 1885.

Verzeichnis der auserlesenen Bücherversammlung des seligen Herrn Moses Mendelssohn. Leipzig, 1926. Brockhaus, Soncino-Gesellschaft.

WALDSTEIN, A. S., *Evolution of Modern Hebrew Literature*. New York, 1916.

WIENER, L., *History of Yiddish Literature in the 19th Century*. New York, 1899.

WÜRDIG, L. and HESSE, B., *Die Dessauer Chronik*. Dessau, 1926–1929.

ZOLLSCHAN, I., *Das Rassenproblem*. Wien, 1912.

INDEX

THE JEWISH PEOPLE

HISTORY · RELIGION · LITERATURE

AN ARNO PRESS COLLECTION

Agus, Jacob B. **The Evolution of Jewish Thought:** From
Biblical Times to the Opening of the Modern Era. 1959

Ber of Bolechow. **The Memoirs of Ber of Bolechow**
(1723-1805). Translated from the Original Hebrew MS. with an
Introduction, Notes and a Map by M[ark] Vishnitzer. 1922

Berachya. **The Ethical Treatises of Berachya, Son of Rabbi**
Natronai Ha-Nakdan: Being the Compendium and the Masref.
Now edited for the First Time from MSS. at Parma and Munich
with an English Translation, Introduction, Notes, etc. by
Hermann Gollancz. 1902

Bloch, Joseph S. **My Reminiscences.** 1923

Bokser, Ben Zion, **Pharisaic Judaism in Transition:** R. Eliezer
the Great and Jewish Reconstruction After the War with Rome.
1935

Dalman, Gustaf. **Jesus Christ in the Talmud, Midrash, Zohar,**
and the Liturgy of the Synagogue. Together with an
Introductory Essay by Heinrich Laible. Translated and Edited
by A. W. Streane. 1893

Daube, David. **The New Testament and Rabbinic Judaism.** 1956

Davies, W. D. **Christian Origins and Judaism.** 1962

Engelman, Uriah Zevi. **The Rise of the Jew in the Western**
World: A Social and Economic History of the Jewish People
of Europe. Foreword by Niles Carpenter. 1944

Epstein, Louis M. **The Jewish Marriage Contract:** A Study
in the Status of the Woman in Jewish Law. 1927

Facets of Medieval Judaism. 1973. New Introduction by
Seymour Siegel

The Foundations of Jewish Life: Three Studies. 1973

Franck, Adolph. **The Kabbalah, or, The Religious Philosophy**
of the Hebrews. Revised and Enlarged Translation [from the
French] by Dr. I. Sossnitz. 1926

Goldman, Solomon. **The Jew and The Universe.** 1936

Gordon, A. D. **Selected Essays.** Translated by Frances Burnce
from the Hebrew Edition by N. Teradyon and A. Shohat,
with a Biographical Sketch by E. Silberschlag. 1938

Ha-Am, Achad (Asher Ginzberg). **Ten Essays on Zionism and**
Judaism. Translated from the Hebrew by Leon Simon. 1922.
New Introduction by Louis Jacobs

Halevi, Jehudah. **Selected Poems of Jehudah Halevi.**
Translated into English by Nina Salaman, Chiefly from the
Critical Text Edited by Heinrich Brody. 1924

Heine, Heinrich. **Heinrich Heine's Memoir:** From His Works,
Letters, and Conversations. Edited by Gustav Karpeles;
English Translation by Gilbert Cannan. 1910. Two volumes in one

Heine, Heinrich. **The Prose Writings of Heinrich Heine.**
Edited, with an Introduction, by Havelock Ellis. 1887

Hirsch, Emil G[ustav]. **My Religion.** Compilation and
Biographical Introduction by Gerson B. Levi. **Including
The Crucifixion Viewed from a Jewish Standpoint:** A Lecture
Delivered by Invitation Before the "Chicago Institute for
Morals, Religion and Letters." 1925/1908

Hirsch, W. **Rabbinic Psychology:** Beliefs about the Soul
in Rabbinic Literature of the Talmudic Period. 1947

Historical Views of Judaism: Four Selections. 1973

Ibn Gabirol, Solomon. **Selected Religious Poems of Solomon Ibn
Gabirol.** Translated into English Verse by Israel Zangwill
from a Critical Text Edited by Israel Davidson. 1923

Jacobs, Joseph. **Jesus as Others Saw Him:** A Retrospect
A. D. 54. Preface by Israel Abrahams; Introductory Essay by
Harry A. Wolfson. 1925

Judaism and Christianity: Selected Accounts, 1892-1962.
1973. New Preface and Introduction by Jacob B. Agus

Kohler, Kaufmann. **The Origins of the Synagogue and
The Church.** Edited, with a Biographical Essay by H. G. Enelow.
1929

Maimonides Octocentennial Series, Numbers I-IV. 1935

Mann, Jacob. **The Responsa of the Babylonian Geonim as a
Source of Jewish History.** 1917-1921

Maritain, Jacques. **A Christian Looks at the Jewish Question.** 1939

Marx, Alexander. **Essays in Jewish Biography.** 1947

Mendelssohn, Moses. **Phaedon; or, The Death of Socrates.**
Translated from the German [by Charles Cullen]. 1789

Modern Jewish Thought: Selected Issues, 1889-1966. 1973.
New Introduction by Louis Jacobs

Montefiore, C[laude] G. **Judaism and St. Paul:** Two Essays. 1914

Montefiore, C[laude] G. **Some Elements of the Religious
Teaching of Jesus According to the Synoptic Gospels.** Being
the Jowett Lectures for 1910. 1910

Radin, Max. **The Jews Amongs the Greeks and Romans.** 1915

Ruppin, Arthur. **The Jews in the Modern World.** With an
Introduction by L. B. Namier. 1934

Smith, Henry Preserved. **The Bible and Islam;** or, The Influence
of the Old and New Testaments on the Religion of Mohammed.
Being the Ely Lectures for 1897. 1897

Stern, Nathan. **The Jewish Historico-Critical School of the
Nineteenth Century.** 1901

Walker, Thomas [T.] **Jewish Views of Jesus:** An Introduction
and an Appreciation. 1931. New Introduction by Seymour Siegel

Walter, H. **Moses Mendelssohn:** Critic and Philosopher. 1930

Wiener, Leo. **The History of Yiddish Literature in the
Nineteenth Century.** 1899

Wise, Isaac M. **Reminiscences.** Translated from the German and
Edited, with an Introduction by David Philipson. 1901